CORPORATIO

CORPORATION TAX

Third edition

H. C. D. RANKIN and D. M. CATTERALL

MACMILLAN

First edition 1977 (published by Gee & Co. Ltd)
Second edition 1985 (published by Van Nostrand Reinhold (UK) Co. Ltd)
Third edition 1989 (published by Macmillan Education Ltd)

Published by
MACMILLAN EDUCATION LTD
Houndmills, Basingstoke, Hampshire RG21 2XS
and London
Companies and representatives
throughout the world

Published in association with the
Institute of Chartered Accountants of Scotland

Typesetting by Footnote Graphics,
Warminster, Wilts

Printed in China

British Library Cataloguing in Publication Data
Rankin, H.C.D. (H. Cunnie D.)
Corporation tax for students.–3rd ed./H.C.D. Rankin and D.M.
Catterall
1. Great Britain. Corporation tax
I. Title   II. Catterall, D.M. (Denise M.)
336.24'3'0941
ISBN 0–333–48808–3 (hardcover)
ISBN 0–333–48809–1 (paperback)

The law is the state-of-the-art as at 13 September 1988.

CONTENTS

PREFACE

This is the third edition of *Corporation Tax*, which was first published over a decade ago. Since that time the book has established itself as a favourite text of students studying for the examinations of accountancy and other professional bodies and those of universities and colleges.

The text of this third edition has been completely revised and updated, much new material being included in the chapters on Capital Allowances (Chapter 2) and the Foreign Element (Chapter 7). As well as a full treatment of the Computation of Profit in Chapter 1 and the Computation and Use of Losses in Chapter 4, Close Companies continue to be fully considered in Chapter 6. Questions of final examination standard are placed at the end of each chapter, and in addition a selection of examination questions (with worked solutions by the authors) from the final examinations of the Institute of Chartered Accountants of Scotland, the Institute of Chartered Accountants in England and Wales, the Institute of Chartered Secretaries and Administrators and the Chartered Association of Certified Accountants are included (Appendixes 3 and 4). We are grateful to these bodies for their permission to use examination questions and other materials published by them.

Members of the accountancy and other professions who are looking for an overview of the principles of corporation tax, written in a clear descriptive style, will find it in this volume.

Many people assisted in the preparation of this edition. Penny Tuck BSc., ACA ATII and Iain Robertson MA, both with Deloitte Haskins & Sells, Cambridge, updated much of the text and statutory references; Janet Rankin MA CA with Price Waterhouse, London, revised chapter and examination questions; Mary Woodley with Rankin & Co., Edinburgh, processed the new texts and material with unfailing good humour and intelligence. These and the many other persons who assisted in various ways have our sincere thanks.

The authors hope that many new readers of *Corporation Tax* will find understanding and examination success by studying this new edition.

H. C. D. Rankin
D. M. Catterall

ABBREVIATIONS

ABA	Agricultural buildings allowance
ACT	Advance corporation tax
AP	Accounting period
BA	Balancing allowance
CA 1985	Companies Act 1985
CAA 1968	Capital Allowances Act 1968
CFC	Controlled foreign company
CGTA 1979	Capital Gains Taxes Act 1979
FA	Finance Act (e.g., Finance Act 1978)
F(2)A 1987	Finance (No.2) Act 1987
FII	Franked investment income
FY	Financial year
FYA	First year allowance
IA	Initial allowance
IBA	Industrial buildings allowance
IDA 1982	Industrial Development Act 1982
OECD	Organisation for Economic Co-operation and Development
Para.	Paragraph (of an Act schedule or an Act section or subsection)
PAYE	Pay-as-you-earn
S. and Ss.	Section and sections (of an Act)
Sched.	Schedule (of an Act)
SLA	Short life asset
TA 1970	Income and Corporation Taxes Act 1970
TA 1988	Income and Corporation Taxes Act 1988
TMA 1970	Taxes Management Act 1970
UFII	Unfranked investment income
WDA	Writing down allowance
WDV	Written down value

CHAPTER 1

THE COMPUTATION OF PROFIT

1.1 INTRODUCTION

Until the passing of FA 1965, the taxation of companies was part of the income tax code which charged both individuals and corporations to tax. In 1965, corporation tax imposed a charge on the profits of companies distinct and separate from the income tax charge on individuals. In addition, when a company distributed profits to its shareholders it paid an additional amount of income tax. This latter feature is a characteristic of what is called the 'classical system' of corporation tax, but since it was shortlived (and in any case something of a novelty in UK taxation when it was introduced in 1965), the significance of the description 'classical system' for our purpose is to distinguish it from the 'imputation system' which was legislated for in 1972, and remains with us.

The classical system made it more expensive to distribute profits than to retain them; the imputation system is in theory neutral as between the taxation of distributed and retained profits, and achieves this by charging all profits of a company at the same rate regardless of the destination of these profits. Neutrality is not, however, always achieved in the practical working out of the system. In both systems one can see very obviously the pre-1965 income tax origins of corporation tax. Even superficially, a corporation tax computation bears the marks of income tax:

A Company Ltd
Corporation tax computation for the year ended 31 March 1989

	£000
Schedule D Case I	500
Schedule D Case III	6
Schedule D Case V	1
Schedule A	2

Unfranked investment income (UFII)	2
Chargeable gains	13
Total profits	524
Less Charges on income	14
Profits chargeable	510
Corporation tax payable: Financial year 1988 35%	178·5

From this, it will be seen that a corporation tax computation retains many of the familiar names and titles of income tax – and, indeed, income tax principles (with important variations) are applied in arriving at the amounts included in each of the schedules of the computation. However, there are differences from income tax; two important differences are the inclusion of 'chargeable gains' in the profit total (these would be taxed under capital gains tax if they arose to an individual taxpayer) and the fact that an assessment on a company is made on its chargeable profits and not under each separate schedule of income, as is the case for income tax.

The imputation system of corporation tax is described in detail in Chapter 3. The system requires that at the time a company pays a dividend it pays to the Inland Revenue an amount of tax, called *advance corporation tax* (ACT). From the company's point of view this payment is, as its name suggests, a payment *in advance* of its ultimate corporation tax liability. When the time comes to compute or pay the corporation tax, for example the figure of £178,500 above, any payment which the company has made in advance – the ACT – is deducted, and only the net amount, the so-called 'mainstream corporation tax' (i.e., what is not paid in advance) is paid to the Inland Revenue. It follows that in the imputation system the payment of a dividend does not increase the amount of the tax payable on a company's profits, but only determines the time at which a part of the corporation tax is paid. This will hold true as long as the distributing company enjoys profits which are charged to corporation tax. If for any reason there are no profits chargeable to corporation tax, so that there is nothing against which to set the ACT, the latter payment may come to have some of the appearances of a tax cost of making distributions in the face of the theoretical basis of the system.

1.2 THE CHARGE TO CORPORATION TAX

Corporation tax is charged on:

(a) companies resident in the United Kingdom,
(b) companies which are not resident in the United Kingdom but which carry on a trade in the United Kingdom through a branch or agency.

The taxation of non-resident companies is dealt with in Chapter 7.

The term 'company' is defined in S.832(1), TA 1988, as any body corporate or unincorporated association. An example of an unincorporated association is a members club, such as a golf club. Much of such a club's income is not taxable in so far as it is what is called 'mutual income' – income which arises from its trading relationships with its members. But where, for example, the club receives interest on bank deposits or other investments, this will be chargeable to corporation tax and not income tax.

1.3 ACCOUNTING PERIODS

Corporation tax assessments are made for *accounting periods* (APs), and are based on the profits of the same APs. This is in contrast to income tax, where assessments are made for fiscal years and are commonly based on the income and profits of business accounts ending in previous fiscal years.

Very often a company's own accounting year is its AP for corporation tax. The basis of assessment for corporation tax may thus be described as a 'current year basis'.

Example 1
Company A Ltd prepares accounts for the 12 months to 31 December 1989. The Inspector of Taxes will make a corporation tax assessment on the profits of A Ltd for the AP commencing on 1 January 1989 and ending on 31 December 1989.

Where the company does not prepare a 12 month account, reference has to be made to the definition of an AP which is provided in S.12, TA 1988:

(1) An AP *begins*:

   (a) when the previous AP comes to an end,
   (b) when a company comes within the charge to corporation tax perhaps for the first time, on becoming resident in the United Kingdom or commencing to trade or acquiring some other source of income (S.12(2), TA 1988).

(2) An AP *ends* on the *earliest* of the following events:
   (a) The expiry of 12 months from the beginning of the AP; – the effect of this is that no AP can be longer than 12 months,
   (b) a date to which the company makes up its accounts,
   (c) the company beginning or ceasing to trade – an illustration of an accounting period ending when a trade begins is given below (Example 2),
   (d) the company beginning or ceasing to be United Kingdom resident,
   (e) the company ceasing to be within the charge to corporation tax – if a company in its lifetime becomes exempt from corporation tax, for example, on becoming a charity, an AP will end at that time.

Apart and distinct from the above rules, an AP ends at the commencement of the winding-up of a company and thereafter annually at the anniversary of the commencement of the winding-up (S.12, TA 1988).

Example 2
On 16 March 1987 Blank Ltd was formed with an authorised share capital of 100,000 ordinary shares of £1 each. On 28 April 1987 the shares were subscribed for and on 2 May 1987 Blank Ltd placed most of the subscription moneys on deposit account with Noland Bank. The company commenced trading on 1 July 1987. Accounts are to be prepared to 30 September each year.

The APs are as follows:

(a) 2 May 1987 to 30 June 1987
   The AP begins on 2 May 1987 when the company acquires a source of income – namely the deposit account (see 1(b) above). The AP ends on 30 June which is the day preceding that on which trading commences (see 2(c) above).
(b) 1 July 1987 to 30 September 1987

This AP begins on 1 July on the day following the end of the previous AP (see 1(a) above).
The AP ends on 30 September, the date to which the company prepares its accounts (see 2(b) above).
(c) Each year to 30 September thereafter will be an AP for corporation tax purposes (see 2(b) above).

Example 3
Cort Ltd commenced trading on 1 July 1984 and made up accounts annually to 30 June. On 1 July 1986 the whole of the share capital of Cort Ltd was acquired by Mar Ltd which prepared accounts to 30 September. It was decided that Cort Ltd would have the same accounting date as its parent company and so accounts were prepared for Cort Ltd for the 15 month period from 1 July 1986 to 30 September 1987 and thereafter to 30 September each year.

The corporation tax APs for Cort Ltd are as follows:

(a) The period of 12 months to 30 June 1985.
(b) The period of 12 months to 30 June 1986.
    In both (a) and (b) the corporation tax AP follows the company's own accounting year. (see 2(b) above).
(c) The period of 12 months to 30 June 1987 – S.12(3)(a) provides that an AP may not exceed 12 months in length (see 2(a) above).
(d) The period of 3 months to 30 September 1987 – the remaining 3 months will form a separate AP which ends on the company's own accounting date (see 2(b) above).
(e) Thereafter each 12 month period beginning with the year to 30 September 1988 (see 2(b) above).

1.4   FINANCIAL YEARS

Corporation tax is charged for financial years at rates which are generally fixed annually in the Finance Act, in arrear. A financial year begins on 1 April in one year and ends on 31 March the next year, and is identified by the year in which it *begins*. The financial year 1987 thus begins on 1 April 1987 and ends on 31 March 1988.

As we have seen, corporation tax assessments are made for specific APs, and in most cases the corporation tax AP will be the same as the period for which the company prepares accounts. If the AP runs from say 1 January 1987 to 31 December 1987, part of the AP is within Financial Year 1986 (i.e., the year from 1 April 1986 to 31 March 1987) and part of the AP is within Financial Year 1987 (i.e., the year from 1 April 1987 to 31 March 1988). In this case, it is necessary to *apportion* the profits of the AP on a *time basis* between the financial years. The rate of tax for each financial year will then be applied to that part of the profits so apportioned (S.8(3), TA 1988).

Example 4

Assume that the accounts of AS Ltd show profits of £360,000 for the year to 31 December 1985 and £540,000 for the year to 31 December 1986. The rates of tax applicable for financial years 1984, 1985 and 1986 are 45%, 40% and 35% respectively.

The corporation tax payable will be calculated as follows:

	£
(i) *AP 1 January 1985 to 31 December 1985*	
Financial year 1984	
(1 January 1985 to 31 March 1985)	
£360,000 × 3/12 = 90,000 at 45%	40,500
Financial year 1985	
(1 April 1985 to 31 December 1985)	
£360,000 × 9/12 = 270,000 at 40%	108,000
Corporation tax payable	148,500
(ii) *AP 1 January 1986 to 31 December 1986*	£
Financial year 1985	
(1 January 1986 to 31 March 1986)	
£540,000 × 3/12 = 135,000 at 40%	54,000
Financial year 1986	
(1 April 1986 to 31 December 1986)	
£540,000 × 9/12 = 405,000 at 35%	141,750
Corporation tax payable	195,750

1.5   COMPUTATION OF PROFITS: Application of Income Tax Principles

S.9, TA 1988 provides that for the purposes of corporation tax, income is to be computed in accordance with income tax principles. This means, for example, that all the statutory and case law rules about allowable deductions in arriving at trading profits for income tax will apply in arriving at Schedule D Case I profits assessable to corporation tax.

Subsection (3) of S.9, TA 1988 puts the matter as follows:

Accordingly for purposes of corporation tax income shall be computed, and the assessment shall be made, under the like Schedules and Cases as apply for purposes of income tax, and in accordance with the provisions applicable to those Schedules and Case, but (subject to the provisions of the Corporation Tax Acts) the amounts so computed for the several sources of income, if more than one, together with any amount to be included in respect of chargeable gains, shall be aggregated to arrive at the total profits.

We would thus expect to find in a corporation tax computation a listing of the company's income taxable under the various schedules and cases. There is given in Appendix 1 a suggested layout for any corporation tax computation, showing not just items dealt with in this chapter but also matters such as loss relief which are dealt with later in the book. You may find it useful to refer to this form while studying the contents of this book – and, indeed, while carrying out any type of corporation tax calculation.

It is not proposed to discuss here all the income tax principles which may apply to companies; readers should refer to any standard work on income tax. There are, however, a number of points which have special significance for corporation tax computations, and these are dealt with below.

1.5.1 Schedule D Case I

Basis of Assessment
As we have seen when considering APs, the basis of assessment for corporation tax is *the profits of the current year*. This is in contrast to the charge to income tax on a continuing business carried on by a sole trader or partnership, where the basis of assessment is the profits for the AP that ended in the *previous fiscal year*.

Interest Payments
In the computation of the Schedule D Case I profits of a sole trader or partnership, all interest is generally allowable as a deduction so long as it is incurred *wholly and exclusively for the purposes of the trade*. As regards bank interest paid by a company, and overdraft interest in particular, this is an allowable deduction for Schedule D Case I purposes. Other interest, such as debenture interest, may be deducted from total profits as a 'charge on income' (see 1.7 below) but is not an allowable expense for Schedule D Case I purposes.

Capital Allowances

The capital allowances to which a company is entitled are calculated in the normal way by reference to CAA 1968 and subsequent Finance Acts (see Chapter 2). For an individual taxpayer capital allowances are deducted *from* the Schedule D Case I profits when charging these profits to income tax. In the case of a company, the capital allowances are normally treated in every respect like trading expenses and are deducted *in arriving at* the Schedule D Case I profit. This apparently small practical difference between the two taxes has a significant effect in certain situations – for example, where losses arise. In the same way, balancing charges arising to a company are treated as trading receipts and are *included* in the Schedule D Case I profits.

Example 5

The accounts of Sunspin Ltd show a net profit of £122,000 after deducting depreciation of £5,000 and debenture interest of £10,000. It is ascertained that the company is entitled to a writing down allowance (WDA) of £3,725. A balancing charge of £2,000 arises on the sale of the managing director's car.

The Schedule D Case I computation will be as follows:

	£	£
Profit per accounts		122,000
Add Depreciation	5,000	
Debenture interest	10,000	15,000
		137,000
Deduct Capital allowances		
WDA		3,725
		133,275
Add Balancing charge		2,000
Schedule D Case I profit		135,275

1.5.2 Schedule D Case III

It is an income tax principle that interest assessed under Schedule D Case III (interest received gross) is the interest *arising in the basis period*. The term 'arising' means the crediting of interest in the taxpayer's account in the books of a bank or other debtor. This income tax principle applies for corporation tax also, and only interest *arising* in the corporation tax AP will be included under

Schedule D Case III in the company's computation of total profits. It follows that any interest which a company may have accrued at the year end is *not* brought into the corporation tax computation.

Example 6
The accounts of Tacker Ltd include a credit of £6,350 in respect of bank deposit account interest. This is made up as follows:

	£
Received in accounting period	6,000
Interest accrued at end of accounting period	350
	6,350

If the net profit shown in the profit and loss account is £100,000, the Schedule D Case I computation will proceed as follows:

	£
Profit per accounts	100,000
Deduct: Deposit account interest	6,350
Schedule D Case I profit	93,650

The Schedule D Case III figure to be included in the corporation tax computation will be £6,000, since this is the amount of interest that arose in the AP.

You will note from Example 6 that the amount of interest which is deducted in arriving at the Schedule D Case I profit is not necessarily the same figure as will be included in the corporation tax computation under the Case III heading.

1.5.3 Income from which income tax has been deducted

Certain types of interest received by an individual – for example, interest from government securities – are received *net of basic rate income tax*. These types of interest, when received by a company, are known as *unfranked investment income* (UFII). The term 'unfranked investment income' is not defined in the legislation, but is commonly used to distinguish such income from franked investment income (FII), which is described below. To say that income is 'unfranked' means that the profits out of which the income has been paid have not been 'franked' or charged to corporation tax. The loan interest or charge on income has been deducted from the total profits of the paying company before arriving at profits chargeable to corporation tax, and is thus paid out of profits *before* tax.

A company in receipt of UFII receives an amount *net of basic rate tax*. It is, however, the *gross* amount of unfranked income that is included in its total profits in the corporation tax computation.

Example 7
In the year to 31 March 1989, Dragon Ltd has adjusted trading profits of £65,000 and receives debenture interest of £750.
The corporation tax computation for Dragon Ltd will take the following form:

	£
	65,000
Schedule D Case I	
UFII $750 \times \dfrac{100}{75}$	1,000
Total profits	66,000

It will be seen that the gross amount of debenture interest of £1,000 has been included in the computation although only £750 was received.

It has been stated earlier that the only tax chargeable on companies is corporation tax. However, in the case of UFII the income has already suffered income tax *by deduction at source*. It follows that some means must be provided to give the company relief for the income tax that has been deducted by the payer.

There are three possible ways whereby the company may obtain this relief:

(a) By setting off income tax suffered against income tax which the company has deducted from loan interest, debenture interest or any other 'charge' which it may have paid during the accounting period (see 1.8 below).

(b) By setting off the income tax suffered against the corporation tax payable for the same AP (see Example 9).

(c) If the two former possibilities are not applicable, the income tax suffered will be repaid to the company, when the corporation tax computation has been agreed with the Inspector of Taxes.

Example 8
We have seen in Example 7 that the total profits of Dragon Ltd for the year ended 31 March 1989 are £66,000.
If we assume a corporation tax rate of 25%, the corporation tax payable by Dragon Ltd will be:

	£
£66,000 × 25%	16,500
Less Income tax suffered by deduction on UFII (£1,000 − £750)	250
Corporation tax payable	16,250

Dragon Ltd has thus obtained relief for the £250 income tax deducted at source from the debenture interest by deducting it from the corporation tax payable.

Example 9
Assume that as a result of utilising trading losses surrendered under the group relief provisions (see Chapter 4) Dragon Ltd has no profits liable to corporation tax.
In these circumstances, there is no corporation tax liability against which to set the income tax suffered and therefore the company will be entitled to have the income tax of £250 repaid (S.7(2), TA 1988).

In certain circumstances, a company may have a corporation tax liability of an amount which is smaller than the amount of the income tax suffered by deduction at source. In this case, the company will obtain *relief* for the income tax suffered:

(a) *firstly* by set off against the corporation tax liability; and
(b) *secondly* by repayment of the balance.

Example 10
Mainsell Ltd receives UFII of £1,500 (net) in its accounting year to 31 March 1989. The gross amount of the UFII (£2,000) will be included in the corporation tax computation, leaving £500 of income tax suffered, for which relief must be obtained.
Mainsell's corporation tax liability for the year to 31 March 1989 has been agreed at £450 (after application of loss relief).
Relief for the income tax deducted from the UFII is obtained as follows:

	£
Income tax suffered	500
Set off against corporation tax liability	450
Balance to be repaid to company	50

You may be aware that bank deposit account interest received by an *individual* is received under deduction of income tax – i.e., net. However, companies receive bank deposit account interest *gross*, and therefore this type of income is not treated as UFII of a company.

1.5.4 Building society interest

When an individual taxpayer receives building society interest, it has to be grossed up at the basic rate of tax for the fiscal year in which the interest is received. The gross sum is then included in the taxpayer's total income for income tax purposes. Similarly, when a company receives building society interest this is treated as having been received net of basic rate income tax. Accordingly when calculating the amount of building society interest to be included in the corporation tax computation the interest received must be grossed up by reference to the basic rate of income tax currently in force. (Multiplied by 100/75 when the basic rate of income tax is 25%.) The credit for the income tax suffered may then be deducted from the corporation tax payable or repaid to the company. The credit *may not* be set against income tax which the company has itself retained under the provisions of Sched. 16, TA 1988 (see 1.7 below).

The possibility of repayment distinguishes the company position from that of an individual. An individual taxpayer cannot receive a repayment of the income tax which is treated as deducted from building society interest (S.476, TA 1988).

1.5.5 Distributions received

Dividends and other distributions received from UK resident companies are not included in the calculation of profits chargeable to corporation tax (S.208, TA 1988). The question of how this income is treated for taxation purposes is dealt with in Chapter 3.

1.6 COMPUTATION OF PROFITS: Application of Capital Gains Tax Principles

The total profits of a company for corporation tax include chargeable gains which if realised by an individual would be charged to capital gains tax. Such chargeable gains are to be computed on the basis of the rules which apply for capital gains tax (S.345(2), TA 1988). Any allowable capital losses will be deducted in arriving at the amount of gains to be included in total profits. Such losses may be losses of the current AP or losses brought forward from earlier APs. Although there are extensive provisions for relieving trading losses, which are described in Chapter 4, the rules for the relief of capital losses are much more restrictive. The company may set off a capital loss against gains of the current AP and may carry forward the balance of the loss for set-off against gains arising in future APs. There are no provisions for set-off of capital losses against any profits other than chargeable gains. Likewise there are no provisions which permit a company to carry back a capital loss for set-off against the chargeable gains of earlier APs.

In the past, chargeable gains of companies were reduced (or 'abated') before being included in a company's total profits. The purpose of the abatement was to apply an effective rate of 30% (the maximum rate of an individual's capital gains tax from 1965 to 1988) when the rate of corporation tax was higher than 30%. The abatement fraction varied over the years as a function of the rate of corporation tax.

Example 11
Morgan Ltd disposed of a chargeable asset in its accounting year to 31 March 1984, and realised a chargeable gain of £10,000.

The computation is:

	£
Chargeable gain	10,000
Less Abatement 2/5	4,000
Abated chargeable gain	£6,000

Corporation tax on chargeable gain is:

6,000 @ 50%	3,000

Note that the tax on the abated chargeable gain (£3,000) is 30% of the unabated chargeable gain.

No abatement applies to gains realised on or after 17 March 1987, and chargeable gains computed on capital gains tax principles have since that date been included in total profits at their full amount.

So far, we have been considering the nature of the total profits of a company for corporation tax purposes. It will, however, be seen from the pro forma in Appendix 1 that certain deductions may be made in calculating the profits chargeable to corporation tax. The deductions, which may be made under the heading 'charges', are considered below.

1.7 CHARGES ON INCOME

Charges are defined as:

(a) any yearly interest, annuity or other annual payment – e.g., royalties;

(b) any other interest paid to a bank, stockbroker or discount house carrying on business in the UK (S.338, TA 1988).

In addition, a non-recurring donation to a charity made on or after 1 April 1986 may, in certain circumstances, be treated as a charge (S.338(2), TA 1988).

The definition of a 'charge' excludes any payment which is deductible as an expense in computing the Case I profit, or any other kind of profit. In particular, bank overdraft interest and bank interest generally is commonly deductible in computing trading profits for the purposes of corporation tax, and in such cases will not be treated as a charge. All other types of interest – for example, debenture interest – will be *added back* in arriving at the Case I liability and will then be deducted from total profits (including the chargeable gains) so long as the interest payments meet certain conditions. The conditions which must be satisfied for the deduction of interest as a charge and for the deduction of any other type of annual payment are briefly as follows:

(i) The charges must be ultimately borne by the company claiming relief for the payment. Thus if a parent company were to debit interest to the receivable account of a subsidiary, the interest could not be said to be 'ultimately borne' by the parent company.

(ii) A charge cannot be deducted from the company's total profits until it has *actually been paid*. Interest in the accounts of a company will commonly include interest accrued or payable. These accrued amounts will not be deductible as charges.

Example 13
In the year ended 30 September 1988 the trading profit in the accounts of Cobber Ltd is arrived at after deducting royalties of £3,000 for the use of certain patented processes. The figure of £3,000 is made up as follows:

	Gross amounts £
Royalties paid in year	2,000
Add Accrued year ended 30 September 1988	2,500
	4,500
Less Accrued year ended 30 September 1987	1,500
	3,000

In computing the amount of the Schedule D Case I profits for the year ended 30 September 1988, the royalties of £3,000 will be *added back*. The amount deductible from total profits under the heading of Charges on Income will be the gross amount of the royalties *actually paid* – i.e., £2,000.

(iii) The definition of a 'charge' includes a covenanted donation to a charity which can continue for more than 3 years – for example, a 4 year deed of covenant. A charitable deed of covenant is broadly an agreement between (say) company A and charity X, whereby company A undertakes to pay the charity a fixed sum for a specified number of years.

A donation to a charity made by a company other than a close company (see Chapter 6) may be treated as a charge even where it is not paid under a deed of covenant. The donation must be paid under deduction of basic rate income tax. There is a maximum amount which may be gifted for the gift to be treated as a charge. The maximum is 3% of the dividends paid on the company's ordinary share capital in the AP in which the donation is made (S.339, TA 1988).

1.7.1 Excess charges

A distinction is frequently drawn in practice between payments of debenture interest, royalties, etc. (called trade charges) and covenanted and non-covenanted donations to charities (called non-trade charges). The importance of this distinction arises when a company pays charges in a particular period which exceed the total profits, leaving a certain amount of charges for that accounting period which can not be utilised at that time.

Example 14
Freedland Ltd is a manufacturing company which prepares accounts to 31 December. In the year 31 December 1988 the company has total profits of £5,000. In the same period the company paid the following charges:

	£
Payments under deed of covenant to charity	6,000
Debenture interest	1,000

The corporation tax computation will proceed as follows:

	£	£
Total profits		5,000
Less: Charges		
Deed of covenant to charity	6,000	
Debenture interest	1,000	
	7,000	
Limited to		5,000
Profits chargeable to corporation tax		Nil

The amount of unrelieved charges £(7,000 − 5,000 = 2,000) is called an 'excess of charges'.

Where there is an excess of charges over total profits the balance can be carried forward and set off against future *trading* profits, but only in so far as the charges were incurred wholly and exclusively for the purposes of the trade. That is to say, only in so far as they are trade charges (S.393(9), TA 1988).

'Trade charges' can thus be carried forward but 'non-trade charges' cannot be carried forward. In this situation, it is clearly beneficial for a company to set non-trade charges paid in a particular AP against the total profits for that AP in priority to trade charges, since the balance of non-trade charges cannot be utilised in future years.

Example 15
In Example 14 Freedland Ltd had unrelieved charges of £2,000 for
the AP ended on 31 December 1988. This figure may be analysed as
follows:

	£	£
Payments under deed of covenant	6,000	
Less: Set against total profits	5,000	
		1,000
Debenture interest		1,000
Unrelieved charges		2,000

The payment under deed of covenant is not a trade charge, and so the
company will be unable to carry forward the unused amount of
£1,000. The company will therefore not obtain relief for this payment.
The debenture interest is a trade charge and so the figure of £1,000
may be carried forward under the provisions of S.393(9), TA 1988.

One further point should be noted regarding the carry forward of
excess charges. In subsequent years, these charges are to be
considered as trading expenses and are set off against trading
profits in arriving at the Schedule D Case I amount; they may *not*
be set against the total profits.

In any corporation tax computation it is thus necessary to
distinguish between charges brought forward and charges paid in
the relevant AP.

Example 16
Greenland Ltd has the following results for the 2 years ended
31 March 1988:

	Year ended 31 March 1987 (£)	*Year ended 31 March 1988* (£)
Adjusted trading profits	1,250	10,000
Chargeable gains	2,000	3,000
Payment under deed of covenant to charity	4,000	4,000
Debenture interest	2,500	2,500

Profits chargeable to corporation tax will be calculated as follows:

Year ended 31 March 1987

	£	£
Schedule D Case I		1,250
Chargeable gain		2,000
		3,250
Less: Charges		
Charity	4,000	
Debenture interest	2,500	
	6,500	
Limited to		3,250
Profits chargeable to corporation tax		Nil

Charges carried forward (S.393(9), TA 1988) £2,500 (note that the unutilised portion of the payment under deed of covenant to charity may *not* be carried forward.

Year ended 31 March 1988

	£	£
Trading profits		10,000
Less: Charges brought forward (S.393(9))		2,500
Schedule D Case I		7,500
Chargeable gains		3,000
		10,500
Less: Charges paid in current year		
Charity	4,000	
Debenture interest	2,500	
		6,500
Profits chargeable to corporation tax		4,000

1.7.2 Deduction of income tax from charges paid

When a company pays debenture interest, royalties or similar charges on income it must deduct income tax at the basic rate for the year in which the payment is made (Ss.349 and 350, TA 1988). The tax which is deducted from the payments made is accounted for in the manner described below.

This procedure of 'deduction of tax at source' is a long-standing method of collection of income tax. In deducting income tax from payments in this way and accounting for that tax to the Inland Revenue, companies are acting as tax collectors.

Example 17
Blueland Ltd is a manufacturing company which prepares accounts to 31 March each year. In the year to 31 March 1989, the company has an obligation to pay debenture interest of £10,000.
On making the payment of £10,000 Blueland Ltd must deduct income tax at the basic rate, and thus £7,500 will go to the debenture holders and £2,500 is accounted for to the Inland Revenue.

It is common, in company accounts and elsewhere, to talk about an amount of charges having been paid, referring to a *gross amount*. You should remember that this gross amount is in two parts: one part which is paid to the individual creditor and the other part which is accounted for to the Inland Revenue. Nevertheless, it is the gross amount which is deducted in the corporation tax computation.

1.8   ACCOUNTING FOR INCOME TAX

We have seen that income tax is deducted at source by companies from payments of loan interest and other charges, and that the income tax is then paid to the Inland Revenue. The arrangements whereby the company notifies the Revenue of the amounts of income tax deducted from each charge, or 'relevant payment' are set out in Sched.16, TA, 1988.
A company makes a return of relevant payments made by it in each *return period*. A return period is:

(a) Each complete quarter of the calendar year falling within the company's AP – i.e., each of the periods of 3 months ending with 31 March, 30 June, 30 September and 31 December.

(b) If the company does not prepare its accounts to a quarter date, then the period from the beginning of the company's own AP to the next quarter date forms a separate return period, and likewise the period from the last quarter date to the end of the company's own AP forms another return period.

Example 18

Accounts are prepared by Fotheringholt Ltd for its year ended 31 August 1988. For Sched. 16, TA 1988 purposes, the return periods will be as follows:

1 September 1987 – 30 September 1987
– period from commencement of accounting period to next quarter date
1 October 1987 – 31 December 1987
– quarterly return period
1 January 1988 – 31 March 1988
– quarterly return period
1 April 1988 – 30 June 1988
– quarterly return period
1 July 1988 – 31 August 1988
– period from last quarter date to end of company's own AP

A company will make a return on a form called a CT61 to the Collector of Taxes within 14 days of the end of each return period, and pay over any income tax which is due within the same time.

The company is liable to pay to the Collector income tax at the basic rate which has been deducted from relevant payments made. However, the company may claim on form CT61 to set off against this income tax any income tax which the company itself has suffered by deduction from its UFII (Para.5, Sched.16, TA 1988).

Example 19

Sumac Ltd prepares accounts to 31 December each year. In the return period running from 1 January 1989 to 31 March 1989, the following transactions take place:

10 February 1989 pays patent royalties (net) of £3,750 (tax deducted £1,250)
26 February 1989 receives debenture interest (net) of £1,500 (tax suffered £500)

Sumac Ltd may set off the income tax suffered of £500 against the income tax of £1,250 which it has deducted from the patent royalties paid on 10 February 1989. The amount of income tax payable to the Collector of Taxes is thus reduced to £750 (i.e., £1,250 *less* £500), payable 14 days after the end of the return period – i.e., by 14 April 1989.

If a company pays income tax to the Collector of Taxes in respect of a relevant payment in one return period and then in a subsequent return period within the same AP it suffers income tax by deduction from UFII which it receives, the company may claim a repayment of income tax on the form CT61.

Example 20

Brinog Ltd prepares accounts to 31 March each year. On 16 April 1988, Brinog Ltd had an obligation to pay loan interest of £9,000. On 17 August it has the right to receive debenture interest of £6,000.

Return period 1 April 1988 – 30 June 1988

A payment of £6,750 is sent to the lender. This represents the £9,000 due *less* income tax of £2,250 (25% of £9,000).

The income tax of £2,250 is paid to the Collector on 14 July 1988.

Return period 1 July 1988 – 30 September 1988

The company is entitled to receive debenture interest of £6,000, but actually receives a payment of £4,500 – being the amount remaining after deduction of income tax (at 25%) of £1,500.

At this point, the overall position is as follows:

	£
Income tax deducted from relevant payments	2,250
Income tax suffered by deduction from debenture interest	1,500
Net amount due to Inland Revenue	750

Since the company paid the Collector £2,250 at the end of the first return period a repayment is made to the company as follows:

	£
Income tax paid to the Collector of Taxes 14 July 1988	2,250
Net income tax due to Revenue	750
Therefore repayment to be made by Collector	1,500

1.9 RATES OF CORPORATION TAX

The rates of corporation tax for the financial years 1983 to 1988 are set out below:

Financial year	Rate of tax (%)	Small company rate (%)	Marginal relief fraction
1983	50	30	1/20
1984	45	30	3/80

Corporation tax for the financial years 1983–8—*continued*

1985	40	30	1/40
1986	35	29	3/200
1987	35	27	1/50
1988	35	25	1/40

1.9.1   Small company rate

It is generally recognised that smaller companies must look to internal sources to finance their development. Because such small companies have limited access to capital (other than those profits which they themselves can generate), the legislation provides in S.13, TA 1988 for a lower than normal rate of corporation tax to be charged on those companies.

If a company has profits (specially defined) of not more than £100,000 for a 12 month AP, then the small company rate is applied to the profits chargeable to corporation tax – in this part of the Taxes Act called the 'basic profits' (S.13, TA 1988).

Profits for the small company rate are defined as profits chargeable to corporation tax plus FII. Any FII which a company receives from a 51% subsidiary and which, if the companies elected, would be group income (see Chapter 5) is ignored – i.e., is not included in the total of FII to be added to chargeable profits (S.13(7), TA 1988).

You will note that the small company rate applies whenever profits are below a certain figure. In the nature of things, small companies will make small profits and will benefit from the reduced rate. But there is no theoretical reason why a large company – or, indeed, a company of any size – should not benefit from the application of the small rate if its profits are not in excess of the limit.

Example 21
Singo Ltd has the following results for the year ended 31 March 1989:

	£
Schedule D Case I	42,500
Schedule D Case III	1,000
Schedule A	2,000
Chargeable gain	1,500
Debenture interest paid	3,000
FII	12,000

The *profits* as defined in S.13(7), TA 1988 are:

	£
Schedule D Case I	42,500
Schedule D Case III	1,000
Schedule A	2,000
Chargeable gain	1,500
Total profits	47,000
Less Charges	3,000
Profits chargeable to corporation tax ('basic profits')	44,000
Add FII	12,000
Profits as defined	£56,000

Since profits for the small company rate do not exceed £100,000, the profits chargeable to corporation tax or basic profits will be charged at the small company rate of 25%:

£44,000 @ 25%   £11,000

Where the AP is less than 12 months, the figure of £100,000 will be proportionately reduced. Thus if the AP of Singo Ltd in Example 21 was 6 months in length, the small company rate would apply only if the 'profits' were less than 6/12 × £100,000 = £50,000.

An *anti-avoidance provision* applies to stop the splitting up of a company's business among several companies in order that each benefits from the lower rate. If a company has one or more associated companies, the limit of £100,000 must be reduced by dividing the limit by 1 plus the number of associated companies that the company has. Thus if a company has 2 associated companies, the small company relief limit becomes:

$$\frac{100,000}{1+2} = \text{£33,333} \quad (\text{S.13(3), TA 1988})$$

For these purposes, one company is an 'associated company' of another if one of them has control of the other, or if both are under the control of the same company or person. Any associated company which has been dormant throughout the relevant accounting period is disregarded.

1.9.2 Marginal small companies relief

We have seen that the small companies rate of corporation tax does not apply to companies whose profits exceed £100,000. In order to lessen the impact of the differential between the small companies rate and the normal rate, S.13(2), TA 1988 provides a method of increasing the rate gradually for companies with profits exceeding £100,000 but less than £500,000.

In order to achieve this graduation, the following method is applied:

(i) Charge the 'basic profits' at the normal full rate.
(ii) Deduct from the corporation tax so computed an amount calculated in accordance with the formula given in the legislation (S.13(2), TA 1988).

For the financial year 1988, the formula is as follows:

$$1/40 \ (M{-}P) \times \frac{I}{P}$$

In this formula:

> M is the 'Upper relevant amount' – i.e., £500,000.
> P is the amount of profits (as defined for the purpose of the small company rate).
> I is the amount of basic profits – chargeable to corporation tax.

Example 22
Pandate Ltd prepares accounts to 31 March each year and the results for the year ended 31 March 1989 are as follows:

	£
Schedule D Case I	230,000
UFII	3,000
Chargeable gain	10,000
FII	40,000
Debenture interest paid	5,000

The total profits liable to corporation tax are:

	£
Schedule D Case I	230,000
UFII	3,000
Chargeable gain	10,000
	243,000
Less Charges	5,000
	238,000

The S.13(7), TA 1988 profits (P) for marginal small companies relief purposes are:

	£
Profits chargeable to corporation tax	238,000
Add: FII	40,000
	278,000

The company's basic profits (I) – profits chargeable to corporation tax – are £238,000

The corporation tax payable is calculated as follows:

	£
£238,000 @ 35%	83,000

Less Marginal small companies relief:

$$1/40 \ (M-P) \times \frac{I}{P} =$$

$$1/40 \ (500,000 - 278,000) \times \frac{238,000}{278,000}$$

	4,751
Corporation tax payable	£78,549

Note:
Although marginal small companies relief has the effect of applying to profits chargeable a corporation tax rate which is less than 35% (in Pandate Ltd above it is

$$\frac{£78,549}{£238,000} = 33\%)$$

you should be aware also of the high marginal rate which applies to Pandate Ltd's chargeable profits in excess of £100,000:

	£
Corporation tax chargeable on profits of £238,000 (as computed)	78,549
Corporation tax chargeable on profits of £100,000 @ 25%	25,000
Corporation tax chargeable on profits in excess of £100,000	£53,549

Rate of charge on Pandate Ltd's chargeable profits in excess of £100,000 is

$$\frac{£53,549}{(£238,000 - £100,000)} = 38.80\%$$

Corporation tax

The high marginal rate of corporation tax on profits between £100,000 and £500,000 has important implications, for example, for group relief (see Chapter 5).

As with the small company rate of corporation tax, there are provisions dealing with APs of less than 12 months and associated companies.

If in Example 22 above the AP of Pandate Ltd were 9 months in length instead of 12 months, the upper relevant maximum amount would become £375,000 (£500,000 × 9/12) and the lower relevant maximum amount would be £75,000 (£100,000 × 9/12).

Again, if Pandate Ltd had 3 associated companies and none was dormant, then the upper and lower relevant maximum amounts applicable for a 12 month AP would become £125,000 (£500,000 divided by [1 + 3]) and £25,000 (£100,000 divided by [1 + 3]).

1.10 DATE FOR PAYMENT OF CORPORATION TAX

In general, the corporation tax assessed for an AP is payable within 9 months of the end of that AP or, if it is later, 30 days from the date of issue of the assessment (S.10(1), TA 1988).

Companies which conducted a trade before 1 April 1965 and which continue in that trade, at one time enjoyed a longer payment interval (up to 21 months) than the usual 9 months. This was because prior to the introduction of corporation tax companies paid income tax under Schedule D Case I, and assessments were normally on a preceding year basis. The 1965/66 income tax assessment on a company (say, X Ltd) with annual accounts ending on 30 June, would thus have as its basis period the year ended 30 June 1964. Income tax charged in this assessment was due on 1 January 1966, and so there was a gap of 18 months between the end of the AP and the payment of tax.

On the introduction of corporation tax in 1965, it was felt to be equitable to provide that where a company conducted a trade and was within the charge to income tax in respect of that trade before 1 April 1965, the same interval of time should elapse between the end of an AP and the due date for payment of corporation tax as lay between the end of the basis period for 1965/66 and 1 January 1966. X Ltd was thus entitled to retain the 18 month gap between the end of its accounting period and the date of payment of corporation tax for so long as it continued to carry on the same trade.

These arrangements gave rise to abuse, and for APs beginning on or after 16 March 1987 the normal payment interval of 9 months applies. However, the change to the new payment date was phased in over 3 years. This was done by dividing the difference between the old payment interval and 9 months by 3. The payment interval for each of the 3 consecutive APs beginning with the AP beginning after 16 March 1987 is then successively reduced by the product of the latter division.

Example 23
An 'old' company makes up accounts to 30 June each year. The payment interval is thus 18 months (see X Ltd above). Dividing the difference between 18 and 9 months by 3 yields 3 months.

AP	Payment interval	Payment date
30 June 1987	18 months	31 December 1988
30 June 1988	15 months (18–3)	30 September 1989
30 June 1989	12 months (15–3)	30 June 1990
30 June 1990	9 months (12–3)	31 March 1991

1.11 GENERAL ADMINISTRATIVE PROVISIONS

The general administrative provisions regarding appeals against assessments to tax and payments to account (S.55, TMA 1970) apply to corporation tax. Where a taxpayer disagrees with the amount of an assessment, he appeals against the assessment within 30 days of the date of issue of the notice of assessment. The appeal will be to the General Commissioners unless the taxpayer elects to bring the appeal before the Special Commissioners. If the taxpayer wishes to postpone all or part of the tax charged by the assessment he must make a claim to the Inspector, again within 30 days of the date of issue of the notice of assessment.

1.12 INTEREST ON OVERDUE CORPORATION TAX

Corporation tax is payable generally 9 months from the end of the relevant AP or 30 days from the date of issue of the notice of assessment, if this is later.

The above dates for payment are called *normal due dates*. Where a company has appealed against an assessment and at the same time claimed to postpone payment of some part of the tax charged, the due date for payment is different for tax postponed and for tax not postponed.

(a) Tax postponed is due after the Commissioners have heard the appeal on the assessment and determined the matter in dispute. An agreement with the Inspector of Taxes after the company has appealed against an assessment has the same force in law as a hearing and determination by Commissioners (S.55(7) and (9), TMA 1970). Following a determination by Commissioners (or its equivalent) the Inspector issues a notice of the tax payable and this is treated from the point of view of due dates for payment as if it were an assessment issued on the date the Inspector issues his notice. This means that corporation tax which is postponed is due 30 days from the date of the notice, if this is later than the normal due date.

(b) As regards the payment to account – i.e., the tax not postponed – this is due 30 days after the Inspector has agreed to the amount to be postponed which is, by corollary, the amount to be paid to account (S.55(6), TMA 1970).

The date from which interest on unpaid corporation tax runs is called the *reckonable date* (S.86(1), TMA 1970). If a company does not appeal against an assessment or appeals against an assessment but does not claim to postpone any of the tax charged, the normal due date is the reckonable date, and interest runs from that date.

If, however, the company appeals against an assessment, and claims to postpone tax, interest on tax postponed and tax not postponed will run from the reckonable date in accordance with the following rule.

Where an appeal has been made with a claim to postponement, the reckonable date is the later of the normal due date which would have applied if there had been no appeal and the earlier of two other dates. The two other dates (of which the earlier is relevant) are the due date (which refers to tax postponed or not postponed) and the 'table date'. The table date for corporation tax is a date 6 months after the 9 months (or longer period for companies trading before 1986) following the end of accounting period (S.86(4), TMA 1970).

Example 24

Moreover Ltd was incorporated in 1970 and makes up its accounts annually to 31 March each year. With respect to the year ended 31 March 1988, the following dates are relevant to the payment of corporation tax and interest on unpaid tax:

Normal due date:	31 December 1988
Table date:	30 June 1989

The company has appealed against an assessment for the accounting period ended 31 March 1988 on which corporation tax payable is £150,000. The company claims to postpone payment of £30,000 of the tax charged; accordingly the tax not postponed, or the payment to account, is £120,000. After correspondence and discussions with the Inspector, the total tax payable on the assessment is agreed at £170,000 and the Inspector issues a notice showing a balance due of £50,000 (£30,000 postponed, plus £20,000 additional tax due).

The relevant dates are as follows:

Date of issue of original assessment	30 November 1988
Date of appeal and claim to postponement	1 December 1988
Date of Inspector's agreement to the amount of tax to be postponed	18 January 1989
Date of issue of notice for balance of tax following agreement with Inspector	12 July 1989

Interest runs from the reckonable dates, which are as follows:

Tax postponed
The due date is 11 August 1989 (30 days from the date of issue of notice for balance of tax). The table date (a fixed date) is 30 June 1989. The earlier date is 30 June 1989.
The reckonable date is the later of the normal due date (had there been no appeal) – 31 December 1988, and the earlier of the due date and table date – 30 June 1989. Since 30 June 1989 is later, this is the reckonable date.

Tax not postponed
The due date is 17 February 1989 (30 days from date of Inspector's agreement – S.55(6)(a), TMA 1970). The table date, as before, is 30 June 1989. The earlier date of these two dates is 17 February 1989. The reckonable date is the later of the normal due date, had there been no appeal – 31 December 1988, and the earlier of the due and table dates, 17 February 1989. 17 February 1989, being later, is the reckonable date.

Additional tax

The balance of the corporation tax due (£50,000) is made up of £30,000, the tax postponed, and an additional amount of tax which was not charged in the notice of assessment issued on 30 November 1988 (£20,000). The reckonable date in the case of the additional tax is to be computed as if the additional tax had been included in the original assessment and postponed. It follows that both the due date for payment and the reckonable date are as for tax postponed, namely 11 August 1989 and 30 June 1989 respectively. This means that we have a somewhat strange situation where interest runs from a date which is earlier than the due date for payment (Ss.55(9) and 86(3)(aa), TMA 1979).

Interest on overdue tax is *not allowable* as a deduction for corporation tax purposes.

1.13 REPAYMENT SUPPLEMENTS

A repayment of corporation tax by the Inland Revenue made more than 12 months after the 'material date' carries with it a *repayment supplement*, which is an amount of tax-free interest (S.825, TA 1988). Interest is paid only for complete tax months and runs from the 6th of the month following the date 12 months after the 'material date'. Tax months begin on the 6th of one month and end on the 5th of the following month (S.825(2), TA 1988). To qualify for a supplement the repayment must be in excess of £100 (S.825(2), TA 1988).

The 'material date' means the normal due date for payment of tax, 9 months from the end of the AP (or longer period in the case of pre-1965 company) (S.825(2), TA 1988).

If corporation tax for an AP was paid more than a year after the material date, interest on a subsequent repayment runs only from the 6th of the calendar month after the next anniversary of the material date.

Example 25

(a) Y Ltd pays corporation tax of £80,000 for the AP ended 31 March 1988 on its normal due date (the material date), 1 January 1989. By reason of a S.393(2), TA 1988 loss claim, £50,000 of the tax for the accounting period ended 31 March 1988 is repaid on 5 August 1990. The £50,000 will be supplemented by a payment of interest in respect of the period 6 January 1990 to 5 August 1990.

(b) If Y Ltd had not paid its £80,000 corporation tax liability until 5 January 1990 (more than 12 months after the material date) no interest supplement would be payable if the repayment was on 5 August 1990 (since interest runs from the next anniversary of the material date).

(c) If, as in (b) above, the corporation tax liability had been paid on 5 January 1990, but the repayment by the Inland Revenue was not made until 5 September 1991, interest would be paid for the period 6 January 1991 to 5 September 1991.

1.14 PAY AND FILE

From 'an appointed day' in the future (which cannot be earlier than 31 March 1992), major changes will occur in the way in which companies make returns and pay corporation tax (Ss.82–95, F(2)A, 1987). This new system is known as 'Pay and File'.

Companies will have to return their profits within 12 months of the end of an AP. Failure to make a return within the prescribed period will give rise to penalties.

Under 'Pay and File', corporation tax will become due and payable 9 months from the end of an AP without the need for the issue of an assessment. In order to avoid payment of interest in a case in which a company has not submitted returns and computations and been assessed to tax within the 9 months following the end of an AP, it will be necessary to estimate and account for the company's tax liability by the due and payable date. Any excess tax later found to have been paid will attract a repayment supplement from the later of the date on which the tax was paid or the due and payable date until the date of repayment.

It is to be noted that payment of corporation tax without the need for any assessment 9 months after the end of an AP is earlier than the obligation, under penalty, to submit a return within 12 months.

Question 1

Exer Sighs Ltd is a company which has been manufacturing keep-fit equipment since 1960. The following is a summary of its profit and loss account for the year ended 31 March 1988:

	£
Trading profit	75,075
Add Other income	9,000
	84,075
Deduct Charges (gross)	7,000
Profit before taxation	£77,075

Notes:

(1) Trading profit was arrived at after charging:

    (a) Directors' fees   £45,000
    (b) Depreciation   £11,625
    (c) Loss on sale of machine   £650

(2) Other income consisted of:

    (a) FII of £2,000 received in September 1987 from a holding of preference shares in Running Boards Ltd.
    (b) Deposit account interest £300.
    (c) Debenture interest of £6,200 (gross) received from Upton Downies Ltd.
    (d) Building Society interest £500.

(3) Charges comprised:
    (a) Annual payment to a charity under a 4 year deed of covenant £2,000.
    (b) Loan interest of £5,000. This is payable in 2 instalments on 30 September and 31 March each year. The payment due on 31 March 1988 was not made until 10 April 1988.

The company disposed of a small office unit on 2 February 1988 and a chargeable gain of £32,000 arises.

The capital allowances for the year ended 31 March 1988 have been calculated at £26,350.

Required:
Calculate the corporation tax payable in respect of the AP ended 31 March 1988, and state the date by which the tax should be paid.

CHAPTER 2
CAPITAL ALLOWANCES

2.1 PRINCIPLES OF CAPITAL ALLOWANCES

The general prohibition against the deduction of capital expenditure in computing Schedule D Case I profits (S.74(f), TA 1988) applies in particular to depreciation charged in a company's accounts. Accounting depreciation traditionally seeks to spread the cost of assets over the years, and is an approximate financial measure of the *physical deterioration of assets* through their limited lives.

In the computation of Schedule D Case I profits for corporation tax purposes, the disallowed accounting depreciation is replaced by a complex and highly detailed system of capital allowances. As previously stated, such allowances are normally treated for corporation tax as trading expenses and if in the operation of the rules a balancing charge arises such a charge is treated as trading income (S.73(2) CAA, 1968).

Capital allowances incorporate two elements: *depreciation proper* of the familiar accounting kind and an *economic element* which seeks to offer an incentive to investment, usually in the form of accelerated rates at which the cost of assets is written off. The allowances are also selective. All assets do not qualify for allowances; and certain assets qualify only if they are of a certain size, or are located in certain parts of the country.

Reliefs for capital expenditure fall broadly into two systems – that instituted in 1945 which provides relief for expenditure on industrial buildings and structures, and that legislated for in 1971 which established the modern framework for reliefs in respect of plant and machinery. Outside of these two systems there exists a wide range of *specific reliefs* for particular kinds of capital expenditure.

Capital allowances for corporation tax, as for income tax, require to be *claimed* (*Ellis* (*Inspector of Taxes*) v. *BP Oil Northern Ireland Refinery Ltd* (STC 1987 52).

The method of computation of allowances and elements of the computation differs as between the industrial buildings and plant and machinery systems. The industrial buildings system employs the 'straight line method' of computing allowances – i.e., a fixed percentage of cost each year; the plant and machinery system adopts the 'reducing balance method' of calculating allowances – i.e., a fixed percentage of the written down value (WDV) of plant and machinery year by year.

2.2 INDUSTRIAL BUILDINGS ALLOWANCES

The industrial buildings system of capital allowances applies to:

(a) Industrial buildings or structures as defined in S.7, CAA 1968, see 2.3 below,
(b) Hotels qualifying for relief in terms of S.38, FA 1978 (expenditure after 11 April 1978), see 2.4 below,
(c) Small and very small workshops, see 2.5 below,
(d) Commercial buildings in enterprise zones (areas designated by the government for special economic incentives), see 2.6 below.

2.3 INDUSTRIAL BUILDINGS OR STRUCTURES

Qualifying Expenditure
CAA 1968 provides relief to companies for expenditure on the construction of an industrial building or structure or in purchasing a new, unused industrial building or structure which is then used in a trade carried on by the company itself or by a tenant or sub-tenant of the company.

'Building or structure' is not defined in the legislation, but an industrial building is among other things a building or structure in use for a trade carried on in a 'mill, factory or similar premises'. The most common type of industrial building qualifying for allowances is thus a factory. However the terms of S.7, CAA 1968 include buildings and structures in use in the following:

(a) Transport, dock, water and power generation activities.
(b) Tunnel and bridge undertakings.

(c) Manufacturing and processing.
(d) Raw materials and finished goods storage (but not by a retailer or wholesaler).
(e) The mineral extraction industry (including the oil industry).
(f) Farming and forestry services.
(g) Agricultural contracting.
(h) The fishing industry.

Structure in the phrase 'industrial building or structure' will include roads, tunnels, walls, car parks, loading platforms, piers and similar structures.

'Building or structure' includes a part of a building or structure, and in this way extensions and improvements to buildings qualify as industrial buildings as expenditure is incurred over the years (S.87(4), CAA 1968). The cost of preparing, cutting, tunnelling or levelling land is regarded as a part of the cost of construction of a building and is available for industrial buildings allowance (IBA). However in no case is expenditure on acquiring the land available for allowances and for the purpose of computing IBA the cost of the land on the one hand and the costs of construction of the building on the other have to be distinguished, see Example 1 below (S.17(1), CAA 1968).

Certain buildings are *excluded* from the definition of an industrial building (and it follows are not granted allowances); these are houses, retail shops and showrooms (S.7(3), CAA 1968).

CAA 1968 also specifies hotels and offices in the list of buildings excluded from the definition of an industrial building. However in certain circumstances such buildings are granted allowances. Expenditure after 11 April 1978 on some hotels qualifies for IBA, see 2.2, 'Qualifying Hotels' below. A drawing office which was ancillary to manufacturing elsewhere in a factory was held in *CIR v. Lambhill Ironworks Limited* (1950) (31TC 393) to be an industrial building. More generally, an office which forms a part of a building may qualify for IBA in the circumstances described below.

Frequently in the construction or purchase of a manufacturing facility there will be included in one building both a manufacturing and a general office area. As a first principle, the cost of constructing the manufacturing area will have allowances available and the office area, assuming it is of a general administrative character, will have no allowances available. Where, however, part of a building is an industrial building and part is not, as long as the cost of construction of the non-industrial part does not exceed 25% of the cost of the construction of the whole, the total costs of construction, including the costs of the non-industrial part, will be available for IBA (S.7(4), CAA 1968).

All welfare premises – for example, a canteen or social club – are to be regarded as industrial buildings if they are used by employees in one of the activities and trades listed in S.7, CAA 1968 which qualify a building as an industrial building, see list above. On the other hand, a sports pavilion used by employees of a trade is an industrial building for the purpose of allowances whether or not the trade is in the qualifying list – e.g., a retail group will obtain IBA in respect of the costs of building a sports pavilion, but not the costs of the employees' social club.

Example 1
Electronics Ltd purchased a five acre site for £30,000 in March 1988 and built a manufacturing unit costing in total £470,000. This cost was made up as follows:

	£
Architect's fees	30,000
Preparing land	50,000
Design office for electronic circuitry	60,000
General office and showroom	100,000
Manufacturing area	200,000
Car parks, roads, walls, gate, etc.	30,000
Total	470,000

The amount available for industrial buildings allowance is as follows:

	£	
Architect's fees	30,000	Costs of construction will
Preparing land	50,000	normally include professional fees (excluding costs associated with acquisition of land), and the costs of preparing, etc. land.
Design office, etc.	60,000	*CIR* v. *Lambhill Ironworks Ltd*
General office, etc.	100,000	Does not exceed 25% of cost of whole building, £470,000 and accordingly an industrial building.

Manufacturing area	200,000	
Car park, etc.	30,000	Structures
Available for IBA	470,000	

The cost of purchasing the land, £30,000, has no allowance available.

2.3.1 Initial allowances

A company incurring expenditure on the construction of a new industrial building was formerly entitled, in the AP in which the expenditure was incurred, to an initial allowance (IA) with respect to that expenditure. A company purchasing a new unused building from a builder was entitled to an IA on the purchase price, and the builder's costs of construction were ignored.

Example 2
Hearts Ltd purchased a new factory from Ace Builders Ltd in Hearts Ltd's AP ended 30 September 1985. The purchase price was £250,000 payable on 31 August 1985. The costs of construction by Ace Builders Ltd were £200,000. Hearts Ltd was entitled to an IA with respect to £250,000 in the AP ended 30 September 1985.

It has been assumed above, and in what follows, that the company incurring the expenditure *itself used the building* in a qualifying trade. A landlord company may also incur expenditure which will qualify for allowances granted to the landlord if the building is used by a tenant in one of the qualifying trades.

It is important to note that the IA was granted only in respect of a *new* building; the purchaser of a used second-hand building obtained no IA.

An IA at various rates was available from 6 April 1944 to 31 March 1986. The rate of IA depended on the date when the expenditure was incurred, which in general terms meant the date when the amount of the expenditure became payable. The IA in respect of expenditure on or after 10 March 1981 and before 14 March 1984 was 75%; in respect of expenditure on or after 14 March 1984 and before 1 April 1985 the allowance was 50%; on or after 1 April 1985 and before 1 April 1986, 25% No IA is granted in respect of expenditure on or after 1 April 1986. The rates of allowances from 6 April 1944 onwards are contained in Appendix 2.

38   *Corporation tax*

For an IA to be given, it was not necessary for the building to be in use; it was sufficient that it would be used subsequently as an industrial building. If subsequently it was not used as an industrial building, any IA given was withdrawn (S.1(5), CAA 1968).

Example 3
Futronic Ltd makes up accounts annually to 31 December. If entered into a contract with a building for the construction of a factory. The contract provided for progress payments, which were made as follows:

	£
Year ended 31 December 1980	75,000
Year ended 31 December 1980	
Pre 10 March 1981	100,000
Post 9 March 1981	90,000
Year ended 31 December 1982	220,000

The building was completed and brought into use in May 1983. IAs available were as follows:

	£
AP ended 31 December 1980	
50% × £75,000	37,500
AP ended 31 December 1981	
50% × £100,000	50,000
75% × £90,000	67,500
AP ended 31 December 1982	
75% × £220,000	165,000

Although the IA is not available from 1 April 1986 it is important to be familiar with it because of its effect in computing the residue of expenditure (see 2.3.5 below).

2.3.2   Writing down allowances

A company which incurs expenditure on the construction of a *new* industrial building (or purchases a *new* industrial building) is entitled to a writing down allowance (WDA) on a straight line basis of 4% (expenditure on or after 6 November 1962) where the building is an industrial building at the end of the AP – i.e., is *in use* for a qualifying trade at the end of the AP. If the expenditure was incurred prior to 6 November 1962 the rate of WDAs is 2% (S.2(1) and (2), CAA 1968). If the AP is less than 12 months in length the allowance is proportionately reduced (Ss.2(2), CAA 1968). Where a company incurs expenditure on a *used* second-hand building the WDA is computed in a special way, see 2.3.6 below, 'Purchase of Second-hand Used Industrial Building'.

Notwithstanding that the WDA is 4% (or 2%) of cost, the amount of an annual WDA cannot exceed the amount of the 'residue' – i.e., the written down value (WDV) of the expenditure – being the cost of the industrial building *less* the IAs and WDAs previously granted (or notional allowances written off, see below). A WDA continues to be given where an industrial building is temporarily disused (S.12, CAA 1968) but not where an industrial building is put to another non-qualifying use – e.g., as a retail outlet. In the latter case – that is, where a building is put to non-qualifying uses – a notional WDA, which is not deducted as a trading expense from trading profits, is deducted in arriving at the residue of the expenditure (S.4, CAA 1968). If notional allowances were not deducted, a balancing allowance (BA) might arise when the building was sold, and in this way an allowance effectively given for years during which it was in use other than as an industrial building; as to BAs see 2.3.3 below.

Example 4
Clubs Ltd, a chemical processing company, constructed a factory costing £300,000 in the early 1970s. In the year ended 30 June 1971 and before the factory was operational it incurred expenditure of £250,000. In the subsequent 6 months' AP ended 31 December 1971 it incurred further expenditure of £50,000. The plant was in operation – i.e., brought into use – at the end of 1971. The IA was 30% throughout the period of expenditure and the company has made up accounts to 31 December annually since the change of accounting date on 31 December 1971. Because of an economic recession, the plant was not in use from 1 September 1979 to February 1984.

IAs and WDAs are as follows:

		(£)	Residue (£)
AP ended 30 June 1971			
IA 30% × £250,000		75,000	175,000
AP ended 31 December 1971			
IA 30% × £50,000		15,000	
(no proportional restriction of initial allowance)			
WDA			
4% × £300,000	£12,500		
Restricted to half		6,000	204,000

Table *continued*

APs ended 31 December 1972 to 1988		
WDAs		
17 years at £12,000 per annum	204,000	Nil
(allowances continue to be		
given during temporary		
disuse)		

Note:
An IA was granted in the AP in which the expenditure was incurred, whether or not the building was in use at the end of the AP. In contrast, WDAs are available only if the building is in use at the end of the relevant AP.

2.3.3   Balancing adjustments

Where an industrial building is sold or demolished (and in other circumstances set out in S.3(1), CAA 1968) a *balancing adjustment* is made. A balancing adjustment may give rise to a deduction from profits or more usually an addition to profits. The object of a balancing adjustment is to allow over the period of use of the building the net cash cost to the company of the capital expenditure.

Example 5
Uno Ltd incurs expenditure on an industrial building costing £300,000. The company obtains allowances over the years of use of the building totalling £300,000. The building is sold for £400,000. The net cash cost to the company is thus nil: it has expended £300,000 and recovered £300,000. Since the net cash cost is nil, the company is not entitled to any allowances and the balancing adjustment will seek to recover tax on the £300,000 of allowances granted over the years of use.
The difference between the selling price of the building (£400,000) and the cost of the building (£300,000), the 'profit' on the sale of the building, is a capital gain.

No balancing adjustment is made where a building is sold more than 25 years after it was first used (50 years if the expenditure was before 6 November 1962). It is important to recall that the definition of an industrial building includes a *part of a building*; it follows that in respect of an industrial building which may be a physical unity, a balancing adjustment may arise with respect to certain expenditure and not arise with respect to certain other expenditure.

Example 6
Spades Ltd, a long established engineering company which makes up accounts to 31 December each year incurred the following expenditure on an industrial building in the years indicated:

	£
Year ended 31 December 1920	50,000
Year ended 31 December 1967	200,000

In the year ended 31 December 1989 the building was sold for £530,000. Of the latter sum £80,000 was in respect of land, and of the balance of £450,000, £150,000 on a just apportionment was attributable to the 1920 expenditure and £300,000 to the 1967 expenditure (Ss.77 and 81, CAA 1968). No balancing adjustment will arise with respect to the £150,000 apportionment to the 1920 expenditure since the 1920 expenditure was more than 50 years before the date of sale in 1989; a balancing adjustment will arise in respect of the 1967 expenditure since the date of sale in 1989 is not more than 25 years after 1967.

If the residue (see 1.3.5 below) exceeds the sale price, a BA is given of the difference (S.3(2), CAA 1968). A BA is deducted from trading income. If the sale price is more than the residue, a *balancing charge* of the difference is made on the company (S.3(3), CAA 1968). A balancing charge is added to trading income. Because of IAs and inflation, balancing charges frequently arise in more common transactions. There is no limit on the amount of a BA, but no balancing charge can exceed the amount of allowances given – i.e., balancing adjustments are intended only to recover any excessive allowances in the past (or to give extra allowances if the allowances have been too low in the past).

Example 7
Diamonds Ltd built a factory in 1966 at a cost of £200,000. The factory was in use (other than temporary disuse for 1 year) from 1966 until it was sold in 1989. The residue of expenditure for IBA purposes at the end of the AP prior to sale was nil; allowances granted to Diamonds Ltd since 1966 were thus £200,000. The sale price of the freehold (the heritage) was £400,000. Diamonds Ltd and the purchaser have agreed that of the £400,000, £100,000 was in respect of land and £300,000 in respect of the industrial building.

The balancing charge arising to Diamonds Ltd on the sale is:

	£	£
Residue before sale		Nil
Sale proceeds:		
Land and buildings	400,000	
Less: Land	100,000	300,000
Balancing charge		300,000
Restricted to allowances granted		200,000

Note:
The excess of the sale proceeds of the land and buildings over the cost of these assets is a capital gain.

2.3.4 Special case of balancing adjustment

When a buiding is sold which at times during its use was an industrial building on which allowances were granted and at other times was not an industrial building – e.g., was in use as retail stores or offices – special rules apply to the balancing adjustment (S.3(4) and (5), CAA 1968).

Where the building is sold for *more* than the building cost, a balancing charge is made which is the amount of the allowances granted.

In the unusual case where the building is sold for *less* than it cost, an adjustment is made to cost, to arrive at what the legislation calls 'adjusted net cost'. If the 'adjusted net cost' is more than the allowances which have been given a BA arises; if less, a balancing charge is made.

'Adjusted net cost' means cost *less* the sale price, reduced in the proportion that the period of time for which allowances were granted bears to the whole period of use.

Example 8
Chess Ltd built a factory at a cost of £300,000 and sold it 4 years later for £250,000. For the first 2 years it was used as a factory and for the last 2 years it was used as a retail outlet. IBAs granted during its years of use as a factory total £174,000.
Since the building was used both as a factory qualifying for IBA and as a retail outlet which does not qualify for allowances the special balancing adjustment is appropriate; the building was sold for less than it cost and the balancing adjustment comprises the difference between adjusted net cost and allowances granted.

Adjusted net cost is as follows:

	£
Cost	300,000
Less: Sale price	250,000
Net cost	50,000
Reduced by factor 2/4	
Adjusted net cost	25,000

Balancing charge is excess of allowances granted over adjusted net cost:

	£
Allowances granted	174,000
Less: Adjusted net cost	25,000
Balancing charge	149,000

2.3.5 Residue of expenditure

Reference was made above to the residue of expenditure which consists of the costs of the industrial building less:

(a) any IA,
(b) WDAs for periods of use,
(c) WDAs for periods of temporary disuse as an industrial building,
(d) notional allowances for periods of use otherwise than as an industrial building.

The so-called 'residue before sale' is the residue as at the end of the AP prior to the AP in which the industrial building is sold. The 'residue after sale' is the residue before sale *plus* the amount of a balancing charge which arises out of the sale or *less* the amount of a BA on the occasion of the sale. The notions of residue, and residue before and after sale, are important when considering balancing adjustments generally, and when computing IBAs available to the purchaser of a second-hand, used industrial building. The position of the latter is considered immediately below.

2.3.6 Purchaser of second-hand used industrial building

The capital allowances which are granted to the purchaser of a second-hand, used industrial building differ greatly from those available to the purchaser (or constructor) of a new, unused building. As emphasised elsewhere in this chapter no IA is available to the purchaser of a used industrial building and the WDA which is annually 4% to the original purchaser is computed in a special way as regards the second-hand purchaser. The purpose of the latter computation is to write off the residue after sale by the 25th year after the building was first used. The computation proceeds as follows:

(a) Establish the 25 year period from the date the building was first used,

(b) Establish the time still to run of the above 25 year period from the date on which the building was sold,

(c) Compute a proportion of the residue after sale (obtained from the seller) which is the length of the AP of the purchaser (usually 1 year) over the period in (b) above. The amount computed is the amount of the WDA.

Example 9

Bridge Ltd makes up its accounts to 31 December each year. On 31 May 1978 in its accounting period ended 31 December 1978 it bought a new unused industrial building from a builder at a cost of £150,000 and brought it immediately into use. The building was used throughout by Bridge Ltd as an industrial building. On 30 November 1985 in the AP of Bridge Ltd ended 31 December 1985 it was sold to Backgammon Ltd in that company's 12 month AP ended 30 September 1986, for a price of £225,000.

The IBA available to Bridge Ltd and the residues before and after sale are as follows:

Bridge Ltd

	£	£
Cost		150,000
AP ended 31 December 1978		
IA 50%	75,000	
WDA 4%	6,000	
	81,000	
AP ended 31 December 1979 to		
AP ended 31 December 1984		
6 years at £6,000 per annum	36,000	117,000
Residue before sale		33,000
Sale price		225,000
Balancing charge		192,000

Restricted to allowances granted	117,000
Residue after sale:	
Residue before sale	33,000
Add: Balancing charge	117,000
	150,000

Backgammon Ltd
No IA will be available to Backgammon Ltd.
The WDA is calculated as follows:

  (a) The 25 year period from the building's first use runs from 1 June 1978 to 31 May 2003.
  (b) The time still to run of the period in paragraph (a) above from the date of sale, 30 November 1985, is 17 years 6 months.
  (c) The proportion of the residue after sale, £150,000, which is the amount of the WDA is:

$$\frac{\text{Length of AP of purchaser}}{\text{Period in (b) above}} = \frac{1 \text{ year}}{17.5 \text{ years}}$$

and the WDA is $\frac{2}{35} \times £150,000 = £8,571$

On a second or subsequent sale of an industrial building the same principles and computations apply, the object being as before to write off the residue which each successive purchaser inherits over the remainder of the 25 year period since the building was first used by the first purchaser or constructor.

Example 10
Backgammon Ltd in Example 9 continues to use the building as an industrial building until it is sold on 28 February 1989 to Cribbage Ltd. Cribbage Ltd, which has made up accounts to 30 June each year, was taken over by the Games Group Ltd on 31 July 1988 and Cribbage Ltd will draw up its accounts to 31 March 1989 and annually to 31 March thereafter. The price paid by Cribbage Ltd for the building was £250,000.

The IBA available to Backgammon Ltd and the residue before and after sale are as follows:

	£
Residue after sale (Bridge Ltd)	150,000
WDAs:	
AP ended 30 September 1986 to	
AP ended 30 September 1988	
3 years at £8,571 (previously computed)	25,713

Residue before sale	124,287
Sale price	250,000
Balancing charge	125,713
Restricted to allowances granted	25,713
Residue after sale:	
Residue before sale	124,287
Add: Balancing charge	25,713
Residue after sale	150,000

The IBAs available to Cribbage Ltd are as follows:

(a) 25 year period as in Example 9 above ends on 31 May 2003,
(b) The time still to run from the date of sale, 28 February 1989, is 14 years 3 months
(c) The proportion of the residue after sale, £150,000, which is the amount of the WDA, is:

$$= \frac{\text{Period in (b) above}}{\text{Length of AP of purchaser}}$$

$$= \frac{9 \text{ months}}{14 \text{ years 3 months}}$$

$$= \frac{9 \text{ months}}{171 \text{ months}}$$

and the WDA is:

$$\frac{9}{171} \times £150,000 = £7,895$$

In the AP of 12 months ending 31 March 1990 and in subsequent years to 31 March the WDA is:

$$\frac{1}{14.25} \times £150,000 - \text{i.e., } £10,526.$$

2.4 QUALIFYING HOTELS

From 1978 onwards, the IBA system was extended, with modifications, to expenditure on qualifying hotels after 11 April 1978. The IA in respect of qualifying hotel expenditure before 1 April 1986 was 20%; after 31 March 1986 the only allowance is the 4% WDA referred to below.

The extension of IBA to hotels was made with caution. It applies only to expenditure after 11 April 1978 and only to hotels which qualify by reason of *size* and *type*. As regards type of hotel, the relief was intended to benefit tourist and not residential hotels; and as regards size the medium-sized and larger hotels were intended to benefit since 10 letting bedrooms were required in order to qualify.

A qualifying hotel has the following characteristics (S.38, FA 1978):

(a) it is open for a minimum of 4 months in a 'season' of 7 months from April to October inclusive,

(b) during the time it is open it has a minimum of 10 letting bedrooms defined as private bedrooms not normally in the same occupation for more than a month,

(c) the services provided normally include breakfasts and evening meals, bed-making and cleaning of rooms.

If a hotel met the above characteristics it obtained a 20% IA on expenditure after 11 April 1978 and before 1 April 1986. The IA applied to the costs of construction or the purchase price of a new hotel; the purchaser of a second-hand, used hotel did not obtain an IA. The costs of an extension or improvements to a qualifying hotel after 11 April 1978 and before 1 April 1986 obtained IAs. Qualifying capital expenditure obtained a 4% per annum WDA.

To establish whether the requirements regarding the number of bedrooms, seasonal opening, etc. are being met (and thus whether allowances are due in respect of certain expenditure) the legislation requires us to look at a period of 12 months which ends, usually, on the last day of the company's accounting period (S.38(4)(a), FA 1978).

Example 11
Scop Ltd, a company in the hotel business, has owned for many years a 50 bedrom tourist hotel open throughout the year. In the company's year to 31 October 1985 the company built an extension containing 6 bedrooms at a cost of £50,000.
Since Scop Ltd satisfied the requirements of a qualifying hotel for the 12 months ended 31 October 1985 (at least 10 letting bedrooms, etc.) it will obtain an IA and a WDA in the year ended 31 October 1985 as follows:

		£
IA	20% × £50,000	10,000
WDA	4% × £50,000	2,000

When a hotel is first used by a company after the beginning of the 12 month period in Example 11, the qualifying period is 12 months from the date of first use:

Example 12
In addition to the extension referred to in Example 11, Scop Ltd, in the year ended 31 October 1985, opens a new tourist hotel on 1 April 1985 which has 30 bedrooms, is open all year round, and cost £400,000. In assessing what IBAs are available for the AP ended 31 October 1985, one is required to look at the characteristics of the hotel for the 12 months since it opened – i.e., the year beginning on 1 April 1985 and ended on 31 March 1986. Since the building meets the requirements of a qualifying hotel for this period, IBA will be available for the AP ended 31 October 1985.

2.4.1 Writing down allowances

The normal WDA, computed on the straight line basis, is available in respect of qualifying hotels. This is granted as in the case of industrial buildings generally, where the hotel is in use at the end of the AP. A WDA continues to be given during temporary disuse as a hotel for 2 years after the end of the accounting period in which the hotel falls temporarily out of use.

2.4.2 Balancing adjustments

Balancing charges and BAs are computed on the sale of an hotel in the same manner as for other industrial buildings, as described earlier in the chapter. A special computation requires to be made 2 years after an hotel ceases to be a qualifying hotel without being sold or disposed of – e.g. by becoming a residential hotel (say) for the elderly. In such an instance, the hotel is deemed to be sold at open market value and a computation made of the resulting balancing charge or BA.

2.5 SMALL AND VERY SMALL WORKSHOPS

As part of a government policy to encourage small businesses certain small industrial buildings, called in S.75, FA 1980 'small workshops', were granted enhanced rates of IA and WDA.
  A FA 1980 small workshop was an industrial building whose

gross internal floor space did not exceed 2,500 square feet. Expenditure on small workshops after 26 March 1980 and before 27 March 1983 qualified for an IA of up to 100% Where part or all of this IA was disclaimed, the company was granted a WDA of 25% on the part disclaimed.

A FA 1982 very small workshop did not exceed 1,250 square feet in gross internal floor area. For expenditure after 26 March 1983, starting where the FA 1980 provisions ended, and before 27 March 1985, the IA and WDA are, as before, up to 100% and 25% respectively.

2.6 ENTERPRISE ZONES

Enterprise zones are geographical areas of the country designated by the government and offering special financial and economic incentives to businesses to develop in these areas. Perhaps the most interesting incentive to businesses is freedom from local authority rates in the designated areas.

From the pont of view of capital allowances and the IBA, expenditure on industrial buildings, qualifying hotels and commercial buildings in enterprise zones is integrated into the IBA scheme with, as for small workshops, an enhanced IA of up to 100% and a WDA of 25%. To qualify the expenditure must have been incurred on contracts entered into within 10 years of the site being included in an enterprise zone (S.74(1), FA 1980).

In addition to industrial buildings and qualifying hotels – i.e., qualifying under FA 1978 as described above – the enhanced IBA applies to commercial buildings or structures. A commercial building or structure is defined in S.74(4), FA 1980, and means a building (other than an industrial building or qualifying hotel) used as an office, or used for the purpose of a trade, profession or vocation. It follows that for practical purposes all business and commercial properties qualify for allowances, including both hotels which obtain allowances as 'qualifying hotels' and those which while not qualifying under FA 1978, satisfy the definition of a 'commercial building'.

By an extra-statutory concession (6 January 1987), a company incurring expenditure on *fixed* plant and machinery which normally obtains a 25% WDA (see 2.7 below) may elect to obtain a

100% IA if the building in which the plant and machinery is a fixture qualifies as explained above.

2.7   PLANT AND MACHINERY

The second major system of capital allowances is that legislated for in 1971 in respect of capital expenditure on plant and machinery.

'Plant and machinery' is not defined in the legislation, and because of the historically higher rates of allowances granted to capital expenditure on plant and machinery (as opposed to that incurred, for example, on buildings), a large number of cases have come before the courts seeking to claim that certain expenditure was incurred on plant and machinery.

In the course of Lord Lindley's judgment in *Yarmouth* v. *France* CA (1887) (19 QBD 647) a workmen's compensation case and not a tax case as such), he said 'There is no definition of plant in the Act; but, in its ordinary sense it includes whatever apparatus is used by a businessman for carrying on his business – not his stock in trade which he buys or makes for sale; but all goods and chattels fixed or moveable, live or dead, which he keeps for permanent employment in his business'.

This dictum had an important influence on subsequent cases. The modern trend in the development of the definition of plant and machinery has been to look at the 'function' of the expenditure – i.e., is the asset part of the apparatus for the carrying on of the business of the company?

The following have been held *to be plant or machinery*:

> Moveable office partitioning
> A dry dock for the repair of ships
> A swimming pool on a caravan site
> A silo for delivering grain
> Special lighting and fittings in licensed premises.

The following have been held *not to be plant and machinery*:

> Prefabricated school buildings
> A canopy over a petrol filling station
> False ceilings to conceal pipes, etc.
> Ship converted as a floating restaurant
> Ordinary light fittings in retail store.

In the nature of things, tax cases tend to consider the more out-of-the-way items of expenditure, although of course they also establish a framework of definitions and principles. Within that framework are to be found all the machinery and equipment of manufacturing industry, as well as furniture and fittings of offices and shops – e.g., desks, counters, chairs, etc. – and motor vehicles such as buses, lorries and cars.

Expenditure on plant and machinery obtains a WDA. For expenditure on or before 31 March 1986, a first year allowance (FYA) was available in addition.

2.7.1 First year allowances

For expenditure after 27 March 1972 and before 14 March 1984 a company could claim an FYA of up to 100%.

After 13 March 1984, allowances were available as follows:

	(%)
After 31 March 1984 and before 1 April 1985	75
After 31 March 1985 and before 1 April 1986	50
After 31 March 1986	Nil

In order for a FYA to be granted, the expenditure had to be incurred wholly and exclusively for the purposes of the trade, and the plant to belong to the company in the AP in which it claimed the allowance. Plant on hire purchase was treated for this purpose as if it belonged to the company.

Within 2 years of the end of the relevant AP, a company was able to disclaim an FYA completely, or specify the reduced amount which it claimed (S.41(3), FA 1971). The reason for this provision was to accommodate claims for FYA with other claims – e.g., for group relief – and generally to permit companies to take best advantage of the allowance.

Expenditure which had available an FYA in an AP did not generally obtain a WDA in the same AP. The balance of the expenditure after writing off the FYA was carried forward and obtained a WDA in the next AP (see 2.7.2 below). For expenditure after 13 March 1984 and before 1 April 1986, the so called 'relevant portion' of capital expenditure available for FYA might also obtain a WDA, but this short term transitional arrangement associated with the ending of the FYA is not discussed here (S.59(4), FA 1984).

An FYA was available for purchases of both new and second-hand plant and machinery. In a few important cases, an FYA was *not* available: motor cars, generally, did not obtain FYAs.

Although motor cars generally did not obtain FYAs, the allowance was granted on expenditure on cars used for *hire to*, or *carriage of*, *members of the public*. A car hire company, or taxi-hire company, thus obtained FYAs in respect of its fleet of cars. By way of contrast, a manufacturing company which purchased cars for its sales force obtained no FYA. Although motor cars were usually denied FYA, it should be emphasised that *lorries* and *vans* obtained FYAs in the usual way.

2.7.2 Writing down allowances

The 1971 legislation, as well as introducing the notion of FYAs, introduced the concept of 'pools' of expenditure on which a WDA of 25% on the reducing balance method would be granted. The idea of a 'pool' where all expenditures are gathered without distinguishing the cost of any particular asset is a helpful one, and has been developed by descriptions such as the 'general pool', the 'car pool', the 'expensive car pool' and the 'short life asset pool'.

A WDA is granted on qualifying expenditure on plant and machinery *less* the disposal value – e.g., sale price of plant and machinery (S.44(2), FA 1971). Qualifying expenditure and disposal value are defined in detail in the legislation (Ss.4, 5 and 6, FA 1971). Simply put, qualifying expenditure *less* disposal value for a given accounting period is made up as follows (see also Example 13 below):

	£
WDV of expenditure which obtained a WDA in the previous AP – i.e., the opening balance of qualifying expenditure	XXX
Balance of expenditure which had available an FYA in the previous AP	XXX
Expenditure in the AP and after	

	XXX
31 March 1986 which did not have available an FYA	XXX
Qualifying expenditure	XXX
Less Sale price (or other disposal value) of plant and machinery sold, etc. in the AP	XXX
Qualifying expenditure *less* disposal value	XXX

The above computation takes place in what is described as the 'general pool', and a similar computation is made in the separate pools described later. Motor cars are not included in the general pool and are subject to separate rules and considerations (see 2.7.5 below). An election to 'de-pool' short life assets (see 2.7.6 below) will exclude the relevant assets from the 'general pool', and these also are subject to special rules. The WDA of 25% is applied to and deducted from 'qualifying expenditure *less* disposal value', to arrive at the WDV which is carried forward to the next AP to form the opening figure in the computation of qualifying expenditure for the next year.

Example 13
DR Ltd makes up accounts to 31 July each year. In the year to 31 July 1986 (in November 1985) it purchased an item of plant costing £75,000. In the year ended 31 July 1987 it purchased machinery costing £10,000 and sold an item of plant for £2,000. The balance of qualifying exenditure at 31 July 1985 was £8,000. The plant and machinery capital allowances computation proceeds as follows:

Capital Allowances Computation

AP ended 31 July 1986	FYAs (£)	General pool (£)	Total (£)
Balance of qualifying expenditure at 31 July 1985		8,000	
Purchase: Plant	75,000		
FYA (50%)	37,500		37,500
WDA		2,000	2,000
Balances at 31 July 1986	£37,500	£6,000	
Capital allowances total – AP ended 31 July 1986			£39,500

Capital Allowances Computation

AP ended 31 July 1986

	FYAs (£)	General pool (£)	Total (£)
Balance of qualifying expenditure at 31 July 1986		6,000	
Balance of FYA expenditure at 31 July 1986		37,500	
Purchase of machinery		10,000	
		53,500	
Sale of plant		2,000	
		51,500	
WDA		12,875	12,875
Balance at 31 July 1987		£38,625	
Capital allowances total – AP ended 31 July 1987			£12,875

Notes:
1. Since the date of the purchase of the plant costing £75,000 was November 1985, the comany has available an FYA of 50% – £37,500 – in the AP ended 31 July 1986. The balance of expenditure obtains a WDA of 25%, by reason of inclusion in the pool, in the next AP – year ended 31 July 1987.
2. Since the date of purchase of the machinery was in the year 1 August 1986 to 31 July 1987, and this is wholly after 31 March 1986, no FYA arises.
3. In working on such computations, you should employ the simple layout suggested below, dealing with the items in the following order:

   (a) opening balances
   (b) additions
   (c) disposals
   (d) allowances
   (e) closing balances

If the AP for which plant and machinery capital allowances is granted is less than 12 months, a proportionately reduced WDA is granted (S.44(2)(a)(ii), FA 1971).

Within 2 years of the end of an AP, a company may disclaim a WDA or specify the reduced amount of the allowance which it claims (S.44(2A), FA 1971).

2.7.3 Disposal value and balancing charge

In the above analysis, the pool of expenditure is arrived at after deduction of the sale proceeds of plant. The 1971 legislation uses the phrase 'disposal value', and S.44(6), FA 1971 provides a description of 'disposal events'. These include sale, demolition or destruction, the permanent loss of the plant, the permanent discontinuance of the trade and 'any other event'.

Where the disposal value is more than the qualifying expenditure (see 2.7.2 above) the difference is called a *balancing charge* (S.44(3), FA 1971). A balancing charge is treated in a corporation tax computation as a trading receipt (S.73(2), CAA 1968).

In no case can the disposal value exceed the capital expenditure incurred in the provision of the plant – i.e., the sale price included in the computation cannot exceed the *cost* of the plant in question. This is an instance where it is necessary to identify the sale of an item of plant with its *purchase*, and the principle of pooling is not followed.

Example 14
Sally's Ltd makes up accounts to 31 March each year. At 31 March 1987 the balance on the pool of qualifying expenditure was £4,000. In the year ended 31 March 1988 the only transaction in plant or machinery was the sale of an item of plant for £6,000 which had cost £5,000 in the year ended 31 March 1986.

The computation for the year ended 31 March 1988 proceeds as follows:

AP ended 31 March 1988

	£
Pool balance at 31 March 1987	4,000
Sale of item restricted to cost	5,000
Balancing charge	1,000

The difference between the selling price of the plant (£6,000) and its cost (£5,000) is a capital gain, and may be taxed accordingly.

2.7.4 Balancing allowances and permanent discontinuance of a trade

No WDAs are given in the year in which a trade is permanently discontinued. The excess, if any, of qualifying expenditure over

the disposal value – e.g., sale proceeds – is allowed as a balancing
allowance.

Example 15

Leonard's Ltd makes up accounts each year to 30 September. The
balance on the pool of qualifying expenditure at 30 September 1987
was £80,000. On 30 June 1988 the company ceased to trade and in the
9 months AP ended 30 June 1988 the company made sales of plant
totalling £40,000 and purchased plant costing £10,000.

AP ended 30 June 1988

		£
Pool balance at 30 September 1987		80,000
Purchases		10,000
		90,000
Sales		40,000
Balancing allowance		50,000

2.7.5 Motor cars

Cars for the purpose of WDAs are divided into two classes, those
costing £8,000 or less and those costing more than £8,000.

Each car costing more than £8,000 is held in a *separate pool*. The
legislation asks us to consider that each car is in use in a separate
trade and that the events of purchase and disposal in the actual
trade take place in the deemed separate trade (Para.10, Sched.8,
FA 1971).

The purpose of these provisions is to restrict the amount of the
WDA in respect of 'expensive' cars to £2,000 per annum, and the
WDA granted is the lesser of 25% of the balance on the separate
pool or £2,000.

On the sale of the expensive car, the separate trade is deemed to
be permanently discontinued and it follows that in most cases an
unrestricted BA arises.

Example 16

Chateau Ltd makes up accounts annually to 30 June. In the year
ended 30 June 1986 the company purchased two cars, Car One costing
£9,000 and Car Two costing £12,000. In the year ended 30 June 1988,
Car one was sold for £4,000 and Car Two for £8,750.

The capital allowance computation proceeds as follows:

AP ended 30 June 1986

	Car One (£)	Car Two (£)	Total (£)
Purchases	9,000	12,000	
WDA at 25% restricted to	2,000	2,000	4,000
Pool balances	7,000	10,000	
Total allowances			4,000

AP ended 30 June 1987

	Car One (£)	Car Two (£)	Total (£)
Pool balance 30 June 1986	7,000	10,000	
WDA at 25%	1,750		1,750
WDA at 25% restricted to		2,000	2,000
Pool balances	5,250	8,000	
Total allowances			3,750

AP ended 30 June 1988

	Car One (£)	Car Two (£)
Pool balance 30 June 1987	5,250	8,000
Sale price	4,000	8,750
BA	1,250	
Balancing charge		750

Cars costing less than £8,000, the second class into which cars are divided, are also kept in a *separate pool*, as if in a separate and distinct trade (S.69, FA 1980). However, unlike the position with expensive cars, *all* cars costing less than £8,000 are kept in one pool and there is no restriction on the 25% WDA. These provisions, tucked away rather oddly in the middle of complex provisions concerning restrictions on FYAs granted to leasing companies, were intended to strike at features of the detailed operation of the pre-1980 rules which the Treasury then regarded as unsatisfactory.

Example 17

Halcyon Ltd in its year ended 31 December 1988 had the following transactions in plant and machinery:

	£
Purchase of lathe (second-hand)	20,000
Purchase of office computer	12,000
Purchase of desk	300
Purchase of Porsche (second-hand)	17,000
Purchase of two Ford Escorts	15,000
Sale of two Ford Cortinas	4,000
Sale of plant	5,000

The balance on the general pool at 31 December 1987 is £8,000 and on the car pool, £1,000. The computation of capital allowances for the AP ended 31 December 1988 is as follows:

AP ended 31 December 1988

	Pool (£)	Car pool (£)	Porsche pool (£)	Total (£)
Pool balances				
31 December 1987	8,000	1,000		
Purchases				
Second-hand lathe	20,000			
Office computer	12,000			
Office desk	300			
Porsche				
Escorts		15,000	17,000	
	40,300	16,000	17,000	
Sales:				
Cortinas		4,000		
Plant	5,000			
	35,300	12,000	17,000	
WDA – 25%	8,825	3,000		11,825
WDA – restricted			2,000	2,000
Pool balances				
31 December 1988	26,475	9,000	15,000	
Total allowances				13,825

2.7.6 Short life assets

For expenditure on plant and machinery it is possible for a company to elect (in writing within 2 years of the end of the AP in which the expenditure was incurred) to have an asset treated as a short life asset (SLA) (S.57, FA 1985). Where an election is made, each SLA is dealt with in a separate pool and on a sale of the asset balancing adjustments, including in particular a BA, as on the cessation of a trade, will arise. An election applies only for 5 years; if the asset is not sold by the end of 4 years from the end of the AP in which an allowance is first granted, the asset is transferred in the next AP to the general pool at its WDV.

Certain assets are not eligible for short life treatment (Sched.15, FA 1985). The most important of these exclusions is *private motor cars*.

Example 18
Typists Ltd purchased a computer for £4,000 and a photocopier for £2,000 in its accounting year ended 30 June 1987. The company elects in writing before 1 July 1989 that both assets be treated as SLAs. In the year ended 30 June 1991, the company trades in the photocopier for £250. On the assumption that the pool of qualifying expenditure at 30 June 1986 was £10,000, the capital allowances computation will proceed as follows:

AP ended 30 June 1987

	General pool (£)	Computer (£)	Photo-copier (£)	Total (£)
Balance 30 June 1986	10,000			
Purchases		4,000	2,000	4,000
WDAs	2,500	1,000	500	
Pool balances	7,500	3,000	1,500	
Total allowances				4,000
AP ended 30 June 1988				
WDAs	1,875	750	375	3,000
Pool balances	5,625	2,250	1,125	
Total allowances				3,000

	General pool (£)	Computer (£)	Photo-copier (£)	Total (£)
AP ended 30 June 1989				
WDAs	1,406	562	281	2,249
Pool balances	4,219	1,688	844	
Total allowances				2,249
AP ended 30 June 1990				
WDAs	1,055	422	211	1,688
Pool balances	3,164	1,266	633	
Total allowance				1,688
AP ended 30 June 1991				
Trade in			(250)	
WDAs	791	316		1,107
BA			383	383
Pool balances	2,373	950		
Total allowances				1,490
AP ended 30 June 1992				
Transfer of computer to general pool	950	(950)		
	3,323			
WDAs	831			831
Pool balance	2,492			
Total allowances				831

Notes:
1. Since the sale of the photocopier is taken into account within 4 years of the year ended 30 June 1987, a BA arises on the cessation of the deemed 'photocopier trade'.
2. Since the computer (the other asset for which an SLA election was made) was not sold by the year ended 30 June 1991, the asset is transferred to the general pool in the following year at its WDV at 30 June 1991.

2.7.7 Hire Purchase

As soon as a hire purchase contract is entered into, and on the assumption that the plant and machinery in question is in use at the end of the AP, WDAs are available on the whole 'cash cost' of the asset, notwithstanding that all the payments under the contract have not been made (S.45, FA 1971).

Example 19
Hamlyn Ltd makes up its trading accounts to 31 December each year. In the year ended 31 December 1987, it acquired an item of plant on hire purchase. The outline of the contract is as follows:

	£
Cash cost of plant	10,000
Deposit 20%	2,000
	8,000
Interest at 10% for 3 years	2,400
Hire purchase price	10,400
Repayable by 36 monthly instalments of $\dfrac{10,400}{36}$ =	288.88

The deposit was paid on 15 November 1987 and the first instalment paid on 15 December 1987.

(a) If the asset is in use in the trade of Hamlyn Ltd at 31 December 1987, the company will obtain a WDA of 25% × £10,000 (cash cost) = £2,500 in the AP ended 31 December 1987.

(b) If the asset is not in use at 31 December 1987, the company will obtain in the AP ended 31 December 1987 a WDA of 25% of the capital payments due and payable at that date:

	£
Deposit	2,000
Capital portion of first instalment $\dfrac{8,000}{36}$	222
	2,222
Whereof 25%	555

2.7.8 Building alterations and machinery demolition

Alterations of buildings incidental to the installations of plant or machinery qualify for plant or machinery capital allowances (S.45, CAA 1968, and Para.15(2), Sched.8, FA 1971).

If a company incurs costs on demolishing plant or machinery which is then replaced by other plant, the cost of the replacement plant or machinery for the purposes of capital allowances is increased by the costs of demolition. If not replaced, the costs of demolition of plant form part of qualifying expenditure in the AP in which the demolition occurs and thus qualify for WDAs (Para.14, Sched.8, FA 1971).

2.7.9 Subsidies and investment grants

In the common case of investment grants payable under Part II, IDA 1982, the amount of the grant is not deducted from capital expenditure for the purposes of capital allowances generally (and other reliefs contained in Part I, CAA 1968).

> **Example 20**
> Hero Ltd in its AP of 12 months ended 31 December 1987 incurred expenditure on a new borer costing £30,000 and obtained a development grant of £6,000.
> The net cost to Hero Ltd of the borer is £(30,000 − 6,000) = £24,000.
> However Hero Ltd obtains a 25% WDA with respect to £30,000.

Other than investment grants under Part II, IDA 1982, subsidies by the Crown or any government or public or local authority are deductible from capital expenditure and only the *net cost* qualifies for allowances (S.84, CAA 1968 and Para.15(5), Sched.8, FA 1971).

Accordingly, selective assistance and regional enterprise grants payable since 1 April 1988 in respect of capital expenditure in the assisted areas in terms of Ss.7 and 8, IDA 1982 require to be deducted from the cost of capital expenditure before calculation of the WDA.

2.7.10 Lessors of plant and machinery

A company whose trade is to lease or hire out assets obtains capital allowances in the normal way. A plant hire company which purchases a mechanical digger which it hires out at a daily rate may thus claim a 25% WDA in respect of its expenditure on the digger. A company which does not trade – say, a property company letting plant in an industrial or commercial building – will also obtain a 25% WDA in respect of expenditure on the plant which it leases. The latter expenditure is pooled separately (S.46(1), FA 1971).

Where a lessee company incurs expenditure on plant and machinery which become landlord's fixtures (say, central heating or lifts) the lessee company is entitled to the benefit of capital allowances, although in law the fixtures do not belong to it (S.59 and Sched.17, FA 1985).

Where a trade is being conducted (including a leasing trade) capital allowances are treated as trading expenses in the corporation tax computation. Allowances given to a non-trading lessor (like the property company above) are given effect to 'by way of discharge or repayment of tax' (S.46(1), FA 1971). The allowances are deducted in the first instance from income from the letting of plant and machinery. If it cannot be wholly relieved against such income in an AP, the company can claim to set off the excess of the relief against total profits of that AP and the preceding AP in a manner similar to, but not identical with, relief for trading losses; any excess relief can also be carried forward for set-off against letting income only, in subsequent APs (S.74, CAA 1968). Relief under S.242, TA 1988 (set-off against a surplus of FII) is also available. The latter relief is fully explained in relation to trading losses and charges in Chapter 4, and applies similarly to these allowances.

For expenditure before 1 April 1986, an FYA in respect of plant and machinery for leasing was denied if certain conditions as to use were not met. The most common condition was that the leased asset would have obtained an FYA had it been purchased by the lessee company. A company leasing a computer to a manufacturing company would thus obtain an FYA because had the manufacturing lessee incurred the expenditure it would have obtained one. On the other hand, a company leasing a car long term to a trading company would not obtain an FYA, because the trading company would not have obtained one had it purchased the car (Ss.64(1) and 98, FA 1980).

2.8 OTHER RELIEFS FOR CAPITAL EXPENDITURE

We have considered earlier in this chapter outlines of the two main reliefs for capital expenditure – the IBA and capital allowances for plant and machinery. We shall look briefly at a further range of reliefs for specific kinds of capital expenditure as follows:

Agricultural land and buildings
Scientific research
Know-how
Patent rights.

In addition to this list there are reliefs for capital expenditure in connection with mines, oil wells and mineral depletion, cemeteries and crematoria, and dredging. These reliefs are not considered here.

Historically, the reliefs which we shall consider were ad hoc reliefs distinct from the mainstream reliefs for industrial buildings and plant and machinery. They are now more closely aligned with the latter reliefs but are still best seen as separate reliefs with special and individual features.

2.9 AGRICULTURAL LAND AND BUILDINGS

A company owning or leasing UK agricultural or forestry land which incurs capital expenditure on buildings and certain other 'works' is granted a WDA of 4% on the straight line basis over a 25 year writing down period (Para.1, Sched.15, FA 1986). 'Buildings' include farmhouses as well as other farm buildings generally, and 'works' include cottages, fences, drainage, sewage works, water and electricity installations, walls, shelter belts of trees, glass houses and reclamation works.

Example 21
MacDuff Ltd, the owner of Birnam Woods, makes up accounts to 11 November each year. In the year ended 11 November 1988 it builds a cattle court at a cost of £40,000. In its AP ended 11 November 1988 and subsequently it will obtain a WDA of £1,600 (being 4% of £40,000).

Where the expenditure is on a farmhouse, one third of the expenditure is the maximum amount available for a WDA (Para.2(2), Sched.15, FA 1986). A farmhouse is the 'building used by the person running the farm' (*Lindsay* v. *IRC* (1953) (34 TC 289)).

2.9.1 Balancing events

When a company sells the land on which there is a qualifying building, a BA or balancing charge does not arise automatically. For agricultural buildings allowance (ABA) the making of BAs and balancing charges requires an *election* to be made jointly by the former and the new owner. The election has to be made in writing to the Inspector of Taxes within 2 years of the end of the AP in which the disposal takes place (Para.7, Sched.15, FA 1986).

BAs and balancing charges are computed in the familiar way by comparing the residue of expenditure (cost *less* WDAs – but no WDA for the year in which the sale takes place) with the sale price. If the sale price *exceeds* the residue a balancing charge arises (limited to allowances previously granted); if the sale price is *less* than the residue a BA is given (Para.6, Sched.15, FA 1986).

2.9.2 Allowances available to new owner

If the election referred to above is made by the former owner and the new owner, the new owner is entitled to a specially computed WDA. The computation is similar to that available to the purchaser of a second-hand used industrial building, described in 2.3.6 above.

The amount on which the allowance is based is the residue of the former owner's expenditure immediately before the sale, increased by the balancing charge (or reduced by the BA) arising on the sale. The latter figure is then divided by what remains at the date of sale of the 25 year writing down period which began at the *beginning* of the first AP for which the allowance was given (Para.7(3), Sched.15, FA 1986).

Example 22
Wheatlands Ltd makes up accounts to 31 March each year. In its year ended 31 March 1987 it incurred qualifying capital expenditure of £60,000. In the year ended 31 March 1990 it sold the farm on 25 December 1989 to Uplands Ltd and £70,000 was the amount apportioned to the relevant capital expenditure. The allowances granted Wheatlands Ltd, the balancing charge on Wheatlands Ltd, and the allowances available to Uplands Ltd are as follows:

Wheatlands Ltd

	(£)	ABA (£)
AP ended 31 March 1987		
Expenditure	60,000	
WDA	2,400	2,400
Residue 31 March 1987	57,600	
ABA AP ended 31 March 1987		2,400

AP ended 31 March 1988 and 1989		
WDAs	4,800	4,800
Residue 31 March 1989	52,800	
ABAs, APs ended 31 March 1988 and 31 March 1989		4,800
AP ended 31 March 1990		
Sale price	70,000	
Balancing charge	17,200	
Restricted to allowances granted £(2,400 + 4,800)	7,200	
Uplands Ltd		
Allowances based on:		
Wheatlands Ltd residue immediately before balancing event	52,800	
Add Balancing charge	7,200	
	60,000	

25 year writing down periods begins 1 April 1987 and ends 31 March 2012.

From 26 December 1989 (following the date of sale) to 31 March 2012 is 22 years 3 months approx. and the WDA available to Uplands Ltd is:

$$\frac{£60,000}{22^{3/12}} = £2,697 \text{ each year}$$

In practice, the computation immediately above would probably be approximated still further, to:

$$\frac{£60,000}{22} = £2,727 \text{ each year}$$

Note:
It is assumed Wheatlands Ltd and Uplands Ltd have jointly elected in terms of Para.7(2), Sched.15 FA 1986 that a balancing event of the kind outlined should occur.

2.9.3 Division of allowances where no balancing event

The effect of electing for a balancing event as described immediately above is that Wheatlands Ltd obtains no allowances (or, rather, it first received them and then had them clawed back by a balancing charge) and Uplands Ltd receives a WDA at a rate in excess of the 4% amount originally available to Wheatlands Ltd! This might not be attractive to Wheatlands Ltd, and it may not wish to sign an election with this effect.

If the seller and purchaser of a relevant interest do not elect for a balancing event, the WDAs are divided between the purchaser and seller.

The seller obtains WDAs of 4% of the agricultural buildings expenditure in the normal way down to the AP in which the sale takes place. In that AP, the allowance is apportioned between the seller and buyer on a time basis (Paras.4(1) and (2), Sched.15, FA 1986). Thereafter, the purchaser receives a 4% WDA (on the original expenditure of the seller) for the remainder of the 25 year writing down period.

Building and other expenditure before 1 April 1986 by a company owning or leasing agricultural or forestry land in the UK was granted an IA of 20% and a WDA of 10% (straight line basis for 8 years). When the land was sold, no balancing adjustments arose to the company incurring the expenditure and the new owner or tenant became entitled to any allowances still to be given.

2.10 SCIENTIFIC RESEARCH

Capital expenditure on scientific research related to a trade carried on by a company is allowed a scientific research allowance of 100% (S.91, CAA 1968).

There are no statutory provisions for disclaiming the allowance or claiming a reduced allowance. In any particular case the alternatives are:

(a) To have the full 100% allowance granted
(b) To seek no allowance
(c) To claim or be granted an IBA or plant or machinery allowance.

Scientific research means 'any activities in the fields of natural or applied science for the extension of knowledge' and includes scientific research which may lead to or facilitate an *extension* of a trade and any medical research specially related to workers' welfare in that trade. Thus if a company manufacturing bagpipes were to incur capital research expenditure into the manufacture of electronic bagpipes this would be of a kind to lead to or facilitate an extension of that company's trade and would, other things being equal, qualify for a scientific research allowance without the company having to show that it was its intention to manufacture such an instrument. Again, a brewery company might incur capital expenditure to undertake medical research into alcoholism among brewery workers, and be allowed the relief.

In order to qualify, the expenditure must be on scientific research from the outset. It is not possible to transfer expenditure made at one time for another purpose (e.g., manufacture) to scientific research at a later time, and claim a scientific research allowance. On the other hand, it is possible to incur capital expenditure on scientific research and claim the allowance and later transfer the assets to another purpose without losing the benefit of the original claim.

As long as the expenditure is capital and the expenditure is on scientific research related to the company's trade, the *nature of the asset* is immaterial.

For expenditure after 31 March 1985, land is not a qualifying asset. However, the proportionate cost of land on the purchase of a building is not thereby excluded from relief. Subject to relieving provisions a dwelling is excluded from relief S.91(1A) and (1B), CAA 1968.

The allowance is granted as a trading expense in the accounting period in which the expenditure is incurred.

When the asset is sold, either

    (a) the excess of the disposal value and the amount of the allowance over the expenditure, or

    (b) the amount of the allowance if less than the excess in (a) is treated as a trading receipt in the accounting period of sale (S.92(2), CAA 1968).

The above somewhat unfamiliar formulations have the same outcome as a balancing charge computation in the context of plant or machinery allowances where the disposal value cannot exceed cost.

Example 23
Scores Ltd, an electronics company, purchased a second-hand building for research into robotics. The cost of the building was £300,000 and a further £50,000 in alterations required by the research project was expended. The expenditure was incurred in the company's AP of 12 months ended 31 December 1981. In the year ended 31 December 1988 the building was sold. We shall consider the taxation implications of a sale of the building for (a) £250,000 and (b) £400,000.

In the AP ended 31 December 1981 the company would be allowed a scientific research allowance of £350,000.

(a) In the year ended 31 December 1988 there would be treated as a trading receipt:

	£
Sale price	250,000
Allowance	350,000
	600,000
Less: Expenditure	350,000
Excess	250,000

(b) In this instance, the amount of the allowance would be treated as a trading receipt:

	£
Sale price	400,000
Allowance	350,000
	750,000
Less Expenditure	350,000
Excess	400,000

The amount of the allowance (£350,000) is less than the above excess of £400,000, and accordingly the amount of the allowance (£350,000) is the amount of the trading receipt.

2.11 KNOW-HOW

A company which purchased 'know-how' before April 1986 for use in its trade was entitled to an annual allowance of one-sixth for 6 years beginning with the AP in which the expenditure was incurred. For expenditure after 31 March 1986 a 25% WDA (reducing balance) is granted and allowances and charges aligned with plant and machinery (S.530, TA 1988).

Know-how is secret industrial information and techniques which either may not be capable of being patented or which it is not desired to patent. Receipts from sales of know-how purchased before 1 April 1986 are treated usually as trading receipts (S.531(1), TA 1988).

Example 24

North Ltd pays £60,000 to South Inc., a US company, for certain secret manufacturing processes. The payment is made in North Ltd's accounting year ended 30 June 1983. North Ltd will be allowed a WDA of £10,000 annually for the years ending 1983 to 1988. In the year ended 30 June 1985, North Ltd sold certain of these processes to Regulus Ltd for £12,000. In its AP ended 30 June 1985, North Ltd will have a trading receipt of £12,000 and North Ltd's allowances continue as before down to 1988. Regulus Ltd will be entitled to a WDA in respect of its purchase.

2.12   PATENT RIGHTS

A company incurring capital expenditure before 1 April 1986 on patent rights to be used in its trade was allowed a WDA over a maximum period of 17 years, which might be reduced if the rights had a lesser number of years to run (S.522, TA 1988). The WDA commenced in the AP in which the expenditure was incurred. For capital expenditure after 31 March 1986, a 25% WDA (reducing balance method) is granted, and BAs and balancing charges given and made as for plant and machinery (S.520, TA 1988).

Question 2

Davy Jones Ltd, which manufactures steel lockers, built an extension to its existing factory between November 1987 and February 1988. The total cost of the project, excluding items eligible for capital allowances as plant and machinery, was £142,000 made up as follows:

	£
Cost of additional land	20,000
Legal fees re above	1,000
Production area	84,000
New drawing office	8,100
Canteen and kitchen	14,600

Toilets	2,200
Works manager's office	6,300
Storerooms	2,800
Architect's fees	3,000
	£142,000

The company makes up its accounts to 31 March annually, and the relevant details relating to IBAs on the factory at 31 March 1987 were:

Year of expenditure	Allowable cost (£)	Residue of expenditure (£)
Year ended 31 March 1959	14,800	4,736
Year ended 31 March 1970	8,600	1,118
Year ended 31 March 1976	12,800	256
Year ended 31 March 1981	2,100	462

In April 1988, the company was acquired by Lockstock and Barrel Ltd, which manufactures safes. Consideration is being given to the transfer of Davy Jones Ltd's activities to the premises of Lockstock and Barrel Ltd, where there is spare capacity. The redundant factory would then be sold. A firm of chartered surveyors has indicated that the whole factory might sell for £400,000.

Required:
1. Calculate the IBA due to Davy Jones Ltd for the year ended 31 March 1988.
2. Prepare notes for a meeting with the accountant of Lockstock and Barrel Ltd to discuss the taxation implications of the possible sale of Davy Jones Ltd's factory, indicating any further information which might be required.

*The Institute of Chartered Accountants of Scotland
Question 8, Part I Examination
September 1983 (amended and updated)*

CHAPTER 3

THE IMPUTATION SYSTEM

3.1 THE PRINCIPLES OF THE IMPUTATION SYSTEM

The imputation system of corporation tax is so called because part
of the corporation tax paid by a company is ascribed or 'imputed'
to shareholders, and is treated as satisfying the basic rate tax
liability on distributions received from the company. The mech-
anics for giving effect to the system are as follows:

(a) When a company distributes profits by way of dividend
(or other so-called 'qualifying distribution'), the company pays to the Revenue a sum called Advance
Corporation Tax (or ACT). The amount of ACT
payable is computed by applying to the amount of the
dividend a fraction which is as follows:

$$\frac{I}{100 - I}$$

where I is the basic rate of income tax for the fiscal year
beginning on 6 April in the financial year in question
(S.14(3), TA 1988).

The ACT fraction or rate for the financial year 1988
(25% being the basic rate of income tax for 1988/89)
thus:

$$\frac{25}{100 - 25} = \frac{25}{75}$$

In the same way, the ACT fraction for the financial year
1987 was 27/73, 27% being the basic rate of income tax for
1987/88.

The fractions are thus determined by the basic rate of
income tax in the corresponding fiscal year. The effect

72

of this is that when the basic rate of income tax is applied to the amount of a dividend plus the related, ACT, the amount so computed is the same as the amount of ACT. There is no *theoretical* reason why in an imputation system of corporation tax the basic rate of income tax and the ACT rate should be related in this way, see 3.11 below.

Example 1
A company pays a dividend of £75,000 in July 1988 when the rate of ACT is 25/75, and the basic rate of income tax, for 1988/89, is 25%.

	£
The amount of the dividend	75,000
Plus the relative ACT 25/75 × £75,000	25,000
Total	100,000
Basic rate income tax of 25% applied to £100,000 is	£25,000

which equals the amount of ACT.

(b) Payments of ACT by a company are what the name suggests: they are payments of corporation tax *in advance* of the normal due dates for payment of the tax. Payments of ACT in respect of distributions made in an AP are deducted (subject to certain restrictions) from the corporation tax charge on the profits of that AP in arriving at the corporation tax liability on the normal due date.

Example 2
The profits chargeable to corporation tax for a company's 12 month AP ended 31 March 1989 are £800,000. The normal due date for payment of corporation tax for the AP ended 31 March 1989 is 31 December 1989. The rate of corporation tax for financial year 1988 is 35%. In July 1988, the company paid a dividend of £57,000 in respect of the year ended 31 March 1988. The rate of ACT for financial year 1988 is 25/75.

AP ended 31 March 1989

Corporation tax payable £800,000 × 35% = £280,000

Advance corporation tax

The rate of advance corporation tax is 25/75. When this is applied to a dividend of £57,000 the result is an amount of ACT of £19,000. The payment of ACT of £19,000 is treated as extinguishing a part of the corporation tax liability for the year in which the dividend is paid, regardless of the year for which it is expressed to be paid.

The amount of corporation tax payable on 31 December 1990 is thus as follows:

Corporation tax payable on 31 December 1989

	£
Corporation tax on profits for year ended 31 March 1989	280,000
Less ACT	19,000
Payable on due date	261,000

The net amount payable on the due date (£261,000) is sometimes called 'mainstream corporation tax'.

(c) A United Kingdom resident person who receives a qualifying distribution from a United Kingdom resident company, receives in addition to the dividend what is called a *tax credit*, which equals the amount of ACT paid by the company on making the distribution. The tax credit is not a sum of money, but (as the name suggests) is a credit which an individual taxpayer can set off against his income tax liability on his total income for the fiscal year in which the dividend is received. An individual is liable to income tax on the amount of the dividend he receives plus the tax credit. Since 'ACT' and 'tax credit' are the same amount, the total on which an individual is charged to income tax is the equivalent of the £100,000 in Example 1.

Example 3

A United Kingdom resident individual receives in January 1989 a dividend of £150 on his holding of ordinary shares in a United Kingdom company. The amount to be included in the income tax computation of the individual is the amount of the dividend – £150 plus a tax credit of 25/75, the rate of ACT for the financial year 1988.

	£
Dividend	150
Tax credit 25/75 × £150	50
	200

Income tax is calculated on the total income of the individual including the dividend plus the tax credit, but the tax credit is set off against his income tax liability for 1988/89. This liability will be arrived at after deducting the personal allowances to which the *individual* is entitled. If in fact the tax payer has no liability to income tax (or a liability which is less than £50), the whole of the tax credit of £50 (or the difference between the income tax liability and £50) is repaid to the taxpayer by the Inland Revenue.

3.2 THE NATURE OF DISTRIBUTIONS

Whenever a company makes a qualifying distribution, it must account for ACT to the Revenue at the appropriate rate. The administrative arrangements for payment of ACT are discussed in 3.9 towards the end of this chapter. Almost all distributions are qualifying distributions. They are not deductible from profits in a corporation tax computation.

The definition of a distribution for the purposes of payment ACT and for corporation tax generally, goes far beyond the payment of an ordinary or preference dividend. The intentions of the legislators in the extensive provisions of Ss.209–211 and 254, TA 1988 are twofold. On the one hand is the intention to prevent profits reaching the taxpayer in a capital form and thus not liable to income tax, and on the other is the intention to prevent 'disguised' dividends reaching shareholders in the shape of interest.

Normally excluded from the definition of distribution for the purposes of corporation tax and ACT are distributions made in respect of shares in the course of the winding-up or liquidation of a company. Such distributions are capital, and from the point of view of a shareholder represent disposals of his shares for capital gains tax purposes (S.209(1), TA 1988).

Most distributions for corporation tax fall into one of three broad categories:

(a) The first category of distribution involves the transfer of cash or other assets of the company to a shareholder. This category includes the normal kind of ordinary or preference dividend.
(b) The second category embraces repayments or reductions of share capital coupled with a bonus issue of shares, before or after the reduction. If the bonus issue

of shares is made after the reduction the amount of the
distribution is the amount treated as paid up on the
bonus issue of shares. If the reduction follows the bonus
issue the amount of the distribution is the reduction.
The second category also includes bonus issues of
redeemable shares or securities. In this instance, the
bonus shares themselves are the distribution.

(c) The third category of distribution consists of interest
payable in exceptional circumstances on loan stock and
debentures. As we have already seen, a payment of
interest is usually a charge on income from which
income tax is deducted at source, and which is deductible from total profits in a corporation tax computation.
The more important distributions included in each of
the three categories are described below.

3.2.1 Distributions of cash or other assets

Dividends, including so-called capital dividends, are *distributions*.
A capital dividend is a dividend which is described as such and
which is paid out of a company's capital profits. The distinction
between a capital dividend and any other kind of dividend has no
significance for taxation.

Generally, any other distribution to shareholders of cash or
other assets of the company will be a distribution for tax.
However, if the shareholders pay in full for the assets transferred
to them if, as the legislation says, the company has received 'new
consideration' for the assets, then there is no distribution. 'New
consideration' is defined in S.254(1), TA 1988, and means
consideration not provided directly or indirectly out of the assets
of the company.

Example 4
(a) ABC Ltd owns 20% of the shares of X Ltd. The shares in X Ltd
are transferred to the shareholders of ABC Ltd and the revenue
reserve of ABC Ltd debited. No payment or other new consideration is given by ABC shareholders for the transfer. Accordingly
the transfer of X Ltd shares to ABC shareholders is a distribution
for tax purposes.
(b) The shares in X Ltd have a market value of 50p per share. If
ABC shareholders were to pay ABC Ltd 50p a share then the
shareholders have provided new consideration equal to the value

of the shares transferred and accordingly the transfer is not a distribution.

(c) In (b) above, the shareholders of ABC paid the full market price for the asset they received from ABC Ltd. If they had paid less than the full market price then S.209(4), TA 1988 provides that the difference between the market value of the asset and the new consideration is a distribution. Thus if they had paid 30p per share when the shares in X Ltd had a market value as before of 50p per share, 20p per share would constitute a distribution.

Example 5
PQR Ltd buys a building from an individual shareholder for £80,000, when the market value of the building is £50,000. The difference between the value of the asset transferred by the company – i.e., cash of £80,000 and the new consideration received by the company, that is the building having a value of £50,000 – is a distribution.
No payment of cash which is a repayment of capital is a distribution.

Example 6
A company has a share capital of 100,000 ordinary shares of £1 all subscribed in cash. In a scheme of reduction of capital the company reduces the shares to 100,000 ordinary shares of 50p and repays 50p on each share. The repayment is not a distribution. From the shareholder's point of view it is a part disposal of his shares for capital gains tax purposes.

The general principle that any transfer of an asset for less than full consideration by a company to a shareholder is a distribution is set aside where the shareholder is the parent, or the fellow subsidiary, of the company making the transfer (S.209(5), TA 1988). For this purpose, a 'subsidiary' is a company of which more than 50% of the ordinary share capital is owned by its parent. Such a subsidiary is called a '51% subsidiary' (S.838, TA 1988).

Example 7
Vax Ltd is the 51 per cent subsidiary of Quad Ltd. Vax Ltd transfers to Quad Ltd at book value of £100,000 a building with a market value of £500,000. Because Quad Ltd is Vax's parent, there is no distribution on the transfer of the building from Vax to Quad for less than full consideration.

3.2.2 Bonus issues coupled with repayment of capital and bonus issues of redeemable capital

A straightforward bonus issue of shares is not a distribution, and as we have seen in Example 6, a repayment or reduction of capital is not a distribution. It is only when a bonus issue is coupled with a repayment of capital that a distribution may arise.

(a) If a company repays ordinary share capital and at the same time or later makes a bonus issue of shares, the amount treated as paid up on the bonus issue is a distribution unless the bonus is declared more than 10 years after the repayment (S.210, TA 1988). A repayment of preference shares is excluded from these provisions. In the case of a closely held family company the '10 year exception' does not apply and a bonus issue at any time following a repayment of capital after 6 April 1965 is a distribution.

Example 8
OPQ Ltd with a share capital of £250,000 in £1 ordinary shares, all subscribed in cash, and a revenue reserve of £80,000 repays 25p on each £1 ordinary share. The repayment of 25p is not a distribution. The total amount repaid is £62,500. Shortly afterwards, OPQ makes a bonus issue of ordinary shares totalling £62,500, debiting revenue reserve with £62,500. A bonus issue of this kind, coupled (as here) with a reduction of capital, is a distribution. Without special legislation, it would be possible for shareholders by this means to receive the revenue reserves of a company in a capital form. Presumably after 10 years the relationship between the reduction and the bonus is too remote to concern the legislators.

(b) A repayment of share capital is not a distribution. However, where a repayment follows an earlier bonus issue of shares made after 6 April 1965, the amount of the repayment is a distribution unless the repayment is made more than 10 years after the bonus issue of capital (S.211, TA 1988). As before, the '10 year exception' does not apply to a closely held family company. A bonus issue of shares preceded or followed by a reduction of share capital may thus give rise to a distribution for tax purposes.

(c) Finally in this category the issue to shareholders or debenture holders of bonus redeemable share capital or bonus securities – e.g., bonus debentures or loan stock – is a distribution. The significant characteristic of this kind of distribution is that the bonus issues are *redeemable*. The amount of the distribution is the amount of the bonus redeemable capital.

Bonus redeemable shares or securities are in the small group of distributions which are 'non-qualifying' for ACT purposes. No ACT is payable in respect of such distributions.

Example 9

A company makes an issue of 50,000 bonus redeemable preference shares of £1 each and debits its revenue reserve with £50,000. The company has made a non-qualifying distribution of £50,000. No ACT is payable by the company. Shareholders in receipt of the bonus shares are liable to higher rate tax only in relation to their respective shares of £50,000. No addition is made for a tax credit since the distribution is non-qualifying.

It has already been seen in (b) above that a repayment of a bonus issue of shares is a distribution. It follows therefore that the redemption of bonus redeemable shares, being a repayment of share capital, gives rise to a further distribution. In the latter case, the distribution is a qualifying one giving rise to a payment of ACT. The legislation in S.233, TA 1988 provides for the set-off of income tax suffered on the issue of the bonus redeemable shares against the tax suffered on the redemption.

3.2.3 Interest payments in certain circumstances

The following is a summary of the more usual cases where interest payable on loan stock or debentures may be found in this third category of distributions:

(a) Interest on bonus redeemable securities of the kind which are themselves distributions,

(b) Interest on debentures or other securities which are convertible into shares or carry a right to receive shares,

(c) Interest which depends to any extent on the results of the company,

(d) Interest which is in excess of a reasonable commercial rate; only the amount in excess of a reasonable commercial rate is a distribution.

The interest payments outlined in paragraphs (a) and (b) above will not generally be treated as distributions where the recipient is a company within the charge to corporation tax. The impact of paragraphs (a) and (b) will thus be restricted to interest payments to shareholders who are individuals.

In addition, interest payments within paragraph (c) will not be treated as distributions where the recipient is a company unless the obligation was entered into before 9 March 1982 (or 1 July 1982 if negotiations had commenced before 9 March 1982), the principal is £100,000 or less, and the principal and interest are repayable within 5 years.

Example 10

A company proposes to accept a loan of £500,000 from a friend of a shareholder. The alternative rates of interest proposed are:

(a) 20% per annum. HM Inspector of Taxes considers that 20% is a reasonable commercial rate.
(b) 25% per annum.
(c) 15% per annum and 30% if profits exceed £40,000.

As regards alternative (a) the whole of the interest paid of 20% is a charge on income deductible from total profits. No part is a distribution.

Since alternative (b) is interest in excess of a reasonable commercial rate the excess interest, 5%, is a distribution. The part of the interest which is considered to be at a reasonable commercial rate, 20%, is a charge on income (S.209(2)(d), TA 1988).

The whole amount of interest paid under alternative (c), 15% – or, when profits exceed £400,000, 30% – is a distribution. This should be contrasted with the position under alternative (b) where only the *excess over a commercial rate* is a distribution.

3.2.4   Purchase by a company of its own shares

A repayment of share capital is not a distribution (S.209(2)(b), TA 1988). If, however, in terms of the Companies Act 1985, a company purchases its own shares, there is, subject to an important exception described below, a distribution of the excess of the purchase price over the amount originally subscribed for the shares.

Example 11

Joy Ltd purchased from S, an individual shareholder, 10,000 of its shares for a sum of £35,000. The original subscription for the shares was £10,000. On the basis that the transaction does not meet the conditions described below, a distribution arises as follows:

	£
Purchase price	35,000
Original subscription	10,000
Distribution	25,000

Since the amount of the distribution, with the addition of the tax credit of one third, is taxed as income in the hands of S, a purchase by a company of its own shares from an individual shareholder is unlikely to be attractive in these circumstances.

In a case where an *unquoted trading company* purchases its own shares from a shareholder, and provided other conditions are satisfied, the purchase will not be a distribution but will be within the normal charge to capital gains tax (Ss.219–229, TA 1988). The other conditions are as follows:

(1) The reason why the company wishes to purchase its own shares must fall into one of two categories:
  (a) a shareholder is faced with an inheritance tax liability arising on a death, and cannot meet this liability without undue hardship unless he sells his shares, or
  (b) the company wishes to purchase its shares wholly or mainly to benefit the trade.

When the legislation was first introduced, there were considerable doubts expressed as to the types of situation in which a company could argue that it wished to purchase its own shares in order to benefit its trade. The Inland Revenue have indicated in a Statement of Practice that they will accept that the purchase of its shares would benefit a company's trade in the following sets of circumstances:

  (i) a dissident shareholder is having an adverse effect on the running of the company's trade,
  (ii) the majority shareholder is retiring to make way for new management,
  (iii) an outside shareholder is withdrawing his investment,
  (iv) the personal representatives of a shareholder who has died do not wish to keep the shares.

In all four circumstances the shareholder would normally be expected to dispose of the whole of his holding.

If the reason for the purchase of the shares is to meet an inheritance tax liability, there are no further conditions to be satisfied. However, if the reason for the purchase is within 1(b) above, the legislation requires a further four main conditions to be satisfied:

(2) The vendor must be resident and ordinarily resident in the United Kingdom in the year of assessment in which the shares are purchased.

(3) In most cases, the vendor must have owned the shares throughout the period of 5 years ending with the date of purchase. Periods of ownership by a spouse will be aggregated with the period of ownership by the shareholder, so long as the shares were transferred by the vendor to this spouse when they were living together.

(4) As a result of the purchase of the shares by the company the vendor's interest in the company must be substantially reduced – i.e., reduced by at least 25%. When considering this condition one must have regard to the holdings of the shareholder's 'associates', such as the vendor's husband or wife and parents or minor children. Where the vendor owns shares in more than one company, there must be a substantial reduction in his interest in the group as a whole.

(5) After the purchase of the shares by the company the vendor must no longer be 'connected' with the company, or any other company in the same 51% group. Broadly, a person will be treated as 'connected' with the company if he, together with his associates, owns more than 30% of the issued share capital.

In the case of both (4) and (5), it should be borne in mind that the Revenue Statement of Practice goes further than the legislation, and envisages that the shareholder will generally dispose of the whole of his holding.

The legislation provides that the purchase of its shares by a company must not form part of a scheme or arrangement which has as one of its main purposes the avoidance of tax (S.219(1), TA 1988).

Where there are doubts about whether a particular transaction satisfies the conditions of S.219, it is possible to apply to the Board of Inland Revenue for clearance (S.225, TA 1988).

3.2.5 Demergers

In another set of circumstances, the legislation has stepped in to prevent what would otherwise be a distribution being so treated. The circumstances are as follows:

Suppose company A owns all the shares of its subsidiary company, B. In A's balance sheet appears an asset which is its shareholding in company B. Suppose then it is desired to 'demerge' company B – that is, it is desired that company B no longer be a subsidiary of company A but have an independent existence, not, it should be stressed, independent of its ultimate owners, the shareholders of company A, but independent of its legal owner, its parent company A. One way to achieve this would be for company A to simply hand over its shares in company B to its (company A's) shareholders pro rata with their shareholding.

Without special relieving provisions, such a transfer would be a qualifying distribution by the company and income in the hands of the shareholders.

However in the above and other similar circumstances S.213, TA 1988 provides that such a distribution will be an 'exempt' distribution – i.e., no ACT is payable and the distribution is not income of the demerging company's shareholder.

The general condition for the application of the relieving provisions is that a company is seeking to demerge its 75% subsidiaries – i.e., those subsidiaries in which it owns 75% or more of the ordinary share capital.

3.3 QUALIFYING AND NON-QUALIFYING DISTRIBUTIONS

All except one of the distributions within the three categories in 3.2 above are qualifying distributions, and require that an amount of ACT should be accounted for. The solitary exception is an issue of bonus redeemable shares or securities – which is a non-qualifying distribution.

There is only one other kind of non-qualifying distribution. This is where a company X receives a non-qualifying distribution of the kind referred to above – say, bonus redeemable preference shares – from company Y in respect of shares which company X holds in company Y. Company X then has an asset (the bonus shares in Y) which it transfers to its shareholders. This transfer in these special circumstances will be a non-qualifying distribution by company X (S.14(2), TA 1988).

3.4 FRANKED INVESTMENT INCOME

A United Kingdom resident person who receives a dividend or other qualifying distribution from a United Kingdom company is entitled to a tax credit. The amount of the credit is equal to the ACT paid by the company in respect of the dividend.

When such a dividend is received by a company the total of the dividend and the tax credit is called *franked investment income* (or FII).

Example 12

VB Ltd prepares accounts to 30 September each year. It received a dividend from a United Kingdom company of £36,000 in August 1988.

Amount of FII:

	£
Dividend received	36,000
Tax credit 25/75 × £36,000	12,000
FII	48,000

FII is so called because the income out of which the dividend has been paid has been charged or 'franked' with corporation tax. The distribution, in short, has been made out of *post-tax profits*. FII should be distinguished from unfranked investment income (UFII – income received by a company from which income tax has been deducted at source) described in 1.5.3.

FII is not charged to corporation tax in the hands of the company receiving it. The income is regarded as having *already suffered* corporation tax.

A company receiving FII is entitled to a tax credit in the same way as an individual, but the uses to which the tax credit may be put are peculiar to companies:

    (a) The tax credit in FII may be set off against the liability of the company to pay ACT on its own qualifying distributions made in the AP in which the FII is received, or in subsequent APs, see 3.5.

    (b) The tax credit may, *in one particular case*, be repaid to the company. This will be discussed in section 4.6.

3.5 FRANKED PAYMENTS

When considering the general principles of the imputation system in 3.1 above, it was seen that a company making a qualifying distribution must account to the Revenue for ACT at the relevant rate on the amount of the distribution. The sum of the distribution plus the ACT is called a *franked payment*.

Example 13
VB Ltd pays a dividend of £105,000 in July 1988.

Amount of franked payment:

	£
Qualifying distribution July 1988	105,000
ACT 25/75 × £105,000	35,500
Franked payment	140,000

ACT may be calculated in one of two ways:

    (a) by applying the appropriate *fraction* to the amount of the dividend; or

    (b) by taking the appropriate *percentage* of the franked payment.

Example 14
In example 13, the two ways in which the ACT could be calculated are:

£
  (a) 25/75 × £105,000 = 35,000
  (b) 25% × £140,000 = 35,000

As noted in 3.1 above:

    (a) The numerator of the ACT fraction is the same as the basic rate of income tax for the corresponding fiscal year – e.g., 25/75 is the ACT fraction for the financial year 1988, and 25% is the basic rate of income tax for 1988/89.

    (b) The numerator of the ACT fraction expressed as a percentage and applied to the amount of a franked payment yields the amount of ACT required.

We have talked above in terms of the company 'accounting to the Revenue for ACT' rather than 'paying ACT'. The reason for the distinction is that the company will not necessarily have to pay to the Revenue the full amount of ACT on the distribution. If the company receives FII during the AP in which the franked payment is made, the FII will be set against the franked payment and the company is required to pay ACT only on the *excess* of franked payments over FII.

Example 15

Assume that the company VB Ltd, which featured in Examples 12 and 13, paid a dividend of £105,000 in July 1988 and received a dividend of £36,000 in August 1988.

The amount of ACT payable on the July distribution is calculated as follows:

	£
Franked payment	140,000
Less FII	48,000
Excess of franked payment over FII	92,000
ACT payable	
£92,000 × 25%	23,000

Note:

It is important that the computation proceeds in this way by setting off FII against franked payments, and not setting off credits against ACT amounts. This is because where the ACT rate changes a computation on the basis of a direct set-off of credits against ACT will yield an *incorrect* answer.

3.6 SET-OFF OF ADVANCE CORPORATION TAX

We have already mentioned in this chapter that ACT is, quite simply, a payment in advance – that is to say, a payment made during, or close to the end of, an AP before the actual corporation tax liability for that AP has been determined. One might expect that the full amount of the ACT paid in respect of a particular AP would as a matter of course be set off against the corporation tax liability as subsequently determined, but this is not always the case. In certain circumstances, the effect of the legislation is to restrict the amount of ACT that may be deducted in arriving at the company's mainstream corporation tax liability.

The nature of the restriction is discussed in 3.6.2, 'Restriction of Advance Corporation Tax Set-off' below.

For APs ending prior to 17 March 1987, the ACT set-off was limited in a further way – to corporation tax on income, with no set-off against corporation tax on chargeable capital gains. For

APs beginning after 16 March 1987, ACT may be set off against the corporation tax liability on the *whole* of a company's profits.

3.6.1 Set-off of advance corporation tax against corporation tax on profits

S. 239, TA 1988 permits the set-off of ACT against a company's liability to corporation tax on its profits.

Example 16
Manvix Ltd has the following results for the AP ended 31 March 1989:

	£
Schedule D Case I	30,000
Chargeable gains	50,000
Charges paid	20,000
Franked payments	30,000
ACT paid	7,500

CT computation for AP ended 31 March 1989

	£
Schedule D Case I	30,000
Chargeable gains	50,000
	80,000
Less Charges paid	20,000
Profits chargeable	60,000
Corporation tax payable:	
£60,000 × 25%	15,000
Less ACT	7,500
Mainstream corporation tax payable	7,500

3.6.2 Restriction of advance corporation tax set-off

As previously mentioned in 3.6 above, there are occasions when the amount of ACT that may be set off against a company's liability to corporation tax on its profits is restricted.

This restriction is dealt with in S.239(2), TA 1988, which states that the maximum ACT set-off permissible is an amount which when added to a qualifying distribution equals the company's profits charged to corporation tax in the period.

Put another way, if the company made franked payments during the AP of an amount equal to its profits then the ACT that would be payable in respect of those franked payments represents the maximum amount of ACT that may be set off against the company's corporation tax liability.

Example 17

Rulers Ltd has income of £600,000 in the year ended 31 March 1989. The company paid a dividend of £750,000 on 10 December 1988 and accounted for ACT of £250,000 on 13 January 1989.
Corporation tax on the profits is:

$$£600,000 \times 35\% = £210,000$$

The maximum ACT that may be set off against the corporation tax liability is calculated as follows:

The profit is £600,000. If the company made franked payments of £600,000 the ACT payable would be £600,000 × 25% = £150,000. The maximum ACT that may be set off under S.239(2), TA 1988 is therefore £150,000.

It can be seen that the restriction contained in S.239(2) can be reduced to a simple rule which will always apply as long as the basic rate of income tax is 25% and the rate of ACT is 1/3.

> *The maximum amount of ACT that can be set off in arriving at a company's mainstream corporation tax liability is an amount equal to 25% of the company's profits.*

The application of this restriction should be considered as a matter of course in any corporation tax computation for a relevant AP. This may be done by looking at two figures:

(a) the profit of the company multiplied by a percentage equal to the basic rate of income tax;

(b) the franked payments made by the company, less the FII for the AP, multiplied by a percentage equal to the basic rate of income tax.

If (a) is greater than (b) then no restriction is called for. If, however, (b) is greater than (a) then there must be a restriction of the amount of ACT that may be deducted in arriving at the mainstream corporation tax liability.

Example 18

The results of Hoppers Ltd for the year ended 31 March 1989 are as follows:

	£
Schedule D Case 1	560,000
Schedule A	5,000
Chargeable gains	20,000
Charges paid	85,000
Franked payments made	555,000
FII received	15,000

CT computation for AP ended 31 March 1989

	£	£
Schedule D Case I		560,000
Schedule A		5,000
Chargeable gains		20,000
		585,000
Less Charges		85,000
Profits chargeable to corporation tax		500,000
Corporation tax payable		175,000
£500,000 × 35%		
Less ACT		
Franked payments	555,000	
Less FII	15,000	
Excess	540,000	
ACT paid by company:		
£540,000 × 25% = £135,000		
ACT set off is restricted to		
£500,000 × 25% = £125,000		125,000
Mainstream corporation tax payable		£50,000

Note:
The company paid ACT of £135,000, but has been permitted to set off only £125,000. There is thus a surplus of ACT of £10,000.

3.6.3 Advance corporation tax rate change during accounting period

Where different rates of ACT apply in different parts of the AP of a company, it is necessary, in calculating the restricted amount of ACT deductible, to apportion the company's profits on a *time basis* to the different parts (S.246(5), TA 1988). The appropriate ACT percentage for each part is then applied to the apportioned income.

Corporation tax

Example 19

Leapers Ltd has profits of £100,000 for its accounting year ended 30 September 1988. The company paid a dividend of £83,750 on 1 July in that year.

The maximum ACT that may be deducted from the corporation tax liability for the AP ended 30 September 1988 is calculated as follows:

Profits apportioned to period 1 October 1987 to 31 March 1988

	(£)	ACT restriction (£)
£100,000 × 6/12 =	50,000	
Amount of restriction £50,000 × 27% =		13,500

Profits apportioned to period 1 April 1988 to 30 September 1988

	(£)	ACT restriction (£)
£100,000 × 6/12 =	50,000	
Amount of restriction £50,000 × 25%		12,500
Maximum ACT set-off		26,000

The company paid a dividend of £81,000 on 1 July 1988 and had to account for ACT of £27,000. Although this amount was paid, only £26,000 may be deducted from the corporation tax liability and the company therefore has surplus ACT of £1,000. The methods whereby this surplus may be used are dealt with immediately below.

3.7 SURPLUS ADVANCE CORPORATION TAX

We have seen that a surplus of ACT arises whenever more ACT has been paid in an AP than it is possible to set against the corporation tax liability for that AP.

There are three ways in which a company can use a surplus of ACT:

(a) In so far as the surplus arises in APs ending on or after 1 April 1984 it may be carried back to APs commencing in the 6 years preceding the AP in which the surplus arises (S.239(3), TA 1988).

(b) The surplus may be carried forward to future accounting periods (S.239(4), TA 1988).

(c) The company may surrender the surplus (or indeed any amount of ACT) to a 51% subsidiary of the company. The meaning of a 51% subsidiary and the nature and consequences of a surrender of advance corporation tax are considered in Chapter 5.

3.7.1 Carry back of surplus advance corporation tax

The surplus may be carried back and set off against the corporation tax liability on the company's profits for APs commencing in the 6 years preceding the AP in which the surplus arises (S.239(3), TA 1988). The surplus is set, as far as possible, against corporation tax for a *more recent* AP before a more remote one. The claim to carry back the surplus must be made within 2 years after the end of the AP in which the surplus arose.

The 6 year period of carry back is available only in respect of a surplus of ACT attributable to an AP ending on or after 1 April 1984. For surpluses arising in APs ending before 1 April 1984, the carry back period is 2 years.

A surplus of ACT which is carried back to an earlier AP will be applied after utilising any ACT which actually was paid in respect of that earlier AP. The restriction on the set-off of ACT applies not only in the AP in which a surplus arises but also in the application of ACT carried back to preceding years (see Example 2).

3.7.2 Carry forward of surplus advance corporation tax

If the company makes no claim to carry the surplus back, or if there remains some unrelieved ACT after it has claimed to carry back under S.239(3), TA 1988, the amount of the surplus, or the amount of the surplus unrelieved, will be carried forward and set off against corporation tax on profits in the next AP. If it cannot be relieved or fully relieved in the next AP it will be carried forward as a surplus to the next AP again, and so on (S.239(4), TA 1988).

Example 20
The following facts concern Trotters Ltd for the 5 years since trading commenced on 1 April 1982:

Years ended	31 March 1985 £	31 March 1986 £	31 March 1987 £	31 March 1988 £	31 March 1989 £
Profits chargeable (all trading income)	75,000	70,000	60,000	30,000	10,000
FII	40,000	40,000	40,000	—	22,000
Franked payments	90,000	90,000	90,000	90,000	25,000
ACT paid	15,000	15,000	15,000	27,000	7,500
CT rate	50%	50%	50%	50%	50%
ACT rate	3/7	3/7	3/7	3/7	3/7

For simplicity, a corporation tax rate of 50% and an ACT rate of 3/7 has been applied for all years.

The first year in which a surplus of ACT arises is the year to 31 March 1988, therefore this is the first year we shall consider.

AP ended 31 March 1988	£	£
Corporation tax payable £30,000 × 50% =		15,000
Less ACT:		
ACT paid year ended 31 March 1988	27,000	
Less Maximum set-off permitted £30,000 × 30%	9,000	9,000
Surplus ACT	18,000	
Corporation tax payable		6,000

The surplus of ACT of £18,000 may be carried back and set off against the corporation tax liability for the three preceding APs.

AP ended 31 March 1987	£	£
Corporation tax payable £60,000 × 50% =		30,000
Less ACT (maximum set-off permitted, £60,000 × 30% = £18,000) ACT paid year ended 31 March 1987	15,000	
Add Surplus ACT from year ended 31 March 1988	3,000	18,000
Corporation tax payable		12,000

AP ended 31 March 1986	£	£
Corporation tax payable £70,000 × 50% =		35,000
Less ACT (maximum set-off permitted £70,000 × 30% = £21,000) ACT paid year ended 31 March 1986	15,000	
Add Surplus ACT from 31 March 1988	6,000	21,000
Corporation tax payable		14,000

AP ended 31 March 1985	£	£
Corporation tax payable £75,000 × 50% =		37,500
Less ACT (maximum set-off permitted £75,000 × 30% = £22,500) ACT paid year ended 31 March 1985	15,000	
Add Surplus ACT from 31 March 1988	7,500	22,500
Corporation tax payable		15,000

Summary of use of surplus ACT arising in year ended 31 March 1988	£	£
Surplus ACT		18,000
Less Utilised in year ended 31 March 1987	3,000	
Utilised in year ended 31 March 1986	6,000	
Utilised in year ended 31 March 1985	7,500	16,500
Surplus ACT still unutilised		1,500

The surplus ACT arising in the year ended 31 March 1988 has been utilised in so far as possible by carry back. There remains a balance unutilised which may be carried forward to future APs.

AP ended 31 March 1989	£	£
Corporation tax payable £10,000 × 50% =		5,000
Less ACT (maximum set off permitted £10,000 × 30% = £3,000) ACT paid year ended 31 March 1989	900	
Add Surplus ACT brought forward from year ended 31 March 1988	1,500	2,400
Corporation tax payable		2,600

3.8 USES OF SURPLUS ADVANCE CORPORATION TAX: ANTI-AVOIDANCE

A company which has a surplus of ACT, perhaps accumulated over some years, has an *asset* which in certain circumstances could be reflected in the value of the company's shares. Suppose company X has experienced many years of successful trading followed by several years of losses and ultimately by a decline in the company's business to the point where the business has become very small. In bad times as well as good the company has declared large dividends, so that in the years when losses were made large surpluses of ACT arose. Company Y which is in the same line of business as company X considers that if it were to buy the shares of X from the present shareholders of that company, so that company X became the wholly owned subsidiary of company Y, it could divert sufficient business from its own activities to make company X profitable again. Against the subsequent corporation tax charge on the profits of company X, company X would be able to offset the surplus of ACT which it is carrying forward from its loss-making years.

The existence of a surplus of ACT in company X in these circumstances effectively reduces the tax burden on company Y's profits. Accordingly, when company Y is considering the purchase price of X Ltd's shares it will pay a price which reflects the value to Y of X's surplus ACT.

To stop the buying and selling of 'surplus ACT companies', S.245, TA 1988 provides that in certain circumstances where there is a change of ownership (as, for example, when X Ltd above becomes a wholly owned subsidiary of Y Ltd), an AP is deemed to end on the date the change-over takes place. No ACT paid on distributions made in APs preceding the change in ownership, including any paid in the deemed AP ending with the change of ownership, can be set off against the corporation tax liabilities of later APs.

S.245, TA 1988 provides that where:

(a) within any period of 3 years there is:
   (i) a change in the ownership of a company, and
   (ii) a major change in the nature or conduct of the company's trade or business, *or*

(b) at any time after a company's business has become small or
negligible and before any revival there is a change of
ownership, surplus ACT from a period before the change of
ownership can be set against corporation tax liabilities only
up to the date of the change of ownership.

Alternative (b) above describes the position of companies X
and Y. Alternative (a) arises where there is a change of
ownership associated with a major change in the nature or
conduct of a company's trade or business.

A major change in the nature or conduct of a trade or business
includes:

(a) a major change in the kind of property dealt in or services or
facilities provided,
(b) a major change in customers, outlets or markets (S.245(4),
TA 1988).

The meaning of a 'major change' is not defined in the legislation.
    The period of 3 years referred to in S.245, TA 1988 means that
as long as the nature or conduct of the trade or business is not
significantly changed until more than 3 years after a change of
ownership, it should still be possible to carry forward pre-change
ACT surpluses. In many cases there will thus be a 3-year
'quarantine'. However, this possibility arises only in the case of
alternative (a).
    A change of ownership is determined in accordance with
detailed rules contained in S.769, TA 1988. A change of ownership
may be usefully thought of as occurring whenever a person
acquires or persons acquire more than half of the ordinary shares
of a company.

3.9 ACCOUNTING FOR ADVANCE CORPORATION TAX

We saw in 1.8 above that for the purposes of accounting for
income tax each AP of a company is divided into quarterly return
periods. The return of dividends and ACT payable is made by
reference to the same return periods, and is made on the same

Revenue form (CT61). As with income tax, the return form and payment of ACT are due 14 days from the end of the return period.

A return on form CT61 will give details of franked payments made during the return period and FII received. As we have seen during this chapter, ACT is payable in respect of the excess of franked payments over FII.

It may be that in some return periods the company makes distributions and therefore pays ACT, while in other return periods it receives FII but does not make franked payments. The general principle is that over the course of the whole accounting period the company should pay ACT only on the *excess* of franked payments over FII. The legislation thus specifies *two* sets of circumstances in which a return on form CT61 must be made:

(a) any return period in which a franked payment is made, and

(b) any return period in which the company receives FII if in an earlier return period in the same AP the company made a distribution and paid ACT (this is because by this means it will be repaid the ACT which has been paid earlier in the accounting period) (Para.4, Sched.13, TA 1988).

If neither of the two sets of circumstances outlined above applies, there is no requirement on the company to make a return.

Example 21
Runners Ltd provides details of the following transactions in its AP ended 31 March 1989:

FII received (inclusive of tax credit):

	£
12 April 1988	3,900
4 June 1988	900
10 October 1988	5,000

Franked payments made:

	£
15 July 1988	50,000

Return period ended 30 June 1988
No return required because no franked payments made. FII received £3,900 is carried forward to next return period.

Return period ended 30 September 1988	£
Franked payment	50,000
Less FII	3,900
	46,100
ACT payable by 14 October 1988	
£46,100 × 25%	11,525

Return period ended 31 December 1988
A repayment of £1,450 arises in this return period and a return, which constitutes the claim to repayment, will be made on Form CT61. The repayment arises because over the whole AP so far the ACT position is as follows:

	£	£
Franked payment		50,000
Less FII		
12 April 1988	3,900	
4 June 1988	900	
10 October 1988	5,000	
	9,800	9,800
		40,200
ACT due so far: £40,200 × 25%		10,050
ACT already paid		11,525
Therefore repay		1,475

Return period ended 31 March 1989
No return required

3.10   SURPLUS FRANKED INVESTMENT INCOME

It has been seen above that FII reduces the corporation tax that has to be paid in advance. It can happen that FII received in an AP exceeds the amount of franked payments. When this occurs, we have what is called a *surplus of FII*. A surplus of FII can be carried forward from one AP to the following AP, and set off against franked payments in that AP. If the surplus plus any FII received in the following AP again exceeds franked payments, the new surplus is carried forward to the next and succeeding APs until the surplus is absorbed by franked payments. A trading loss may in certain circumstances be relieved by set-off against a surplus of FII. This relief is dealt with in 4.6 below.

A surplus of FII may not be carried back to earlier APs.

Example 22
The following facts refer to Riders Ltd for the years stated:

Years ended	31 March 1988 (£)	31 March 1989 (£)
Schedule D Case 1 (trading income)	60,000	80,000
FII	12,000	15,000
Dividends paid	—	18,000
Corporation tax rate	35%	35%
ACT rate	29/71	1/3

Note:
FII *by definition* is the amount of dividends received plus tax credit. FII for both years is accordingly the 'gross amount' of such income, which is found by applying the relevant ACT rate for each respective financial year.
Dividends *by definition* are qualifying distributions. Franked payments are qualifying distributions plus ACT. Dividends for the year ended 31 March 1989 are thus the 'net amounts' of those payments.

AP ended 31 March 1988	£	£
FII		12,000
Franked payments		Nil
Surplus of FII carried forward		12,000
Corporation tax payable: £60,000 × 35% =		21,000

AP ended 31 March 1989		
Surplus of FII brought forward		12,000
FII		15,000
		27,000
Franked payments:		
Dividends	18,000	
Add ACT at 1/3 × £18,000	6,000	
Franked payment	24,000	24,000
Surplus of FII carried forward		3,000
Corporation tax payable: £80,000 × 35%		28,000

It will be observed that the tax credit that becomes available when a qualifying distribution is received by a company affords no ultimate relief from corporation tax. The benefit obtained by a company consists in not having to pay corporation tax in advance. Corporation tax is charged with reference to *profits chargeable*, which are unaltered either by dividends received or dividends paid. You will remember that FII is not included in profits of a company for tax purposes.

3.11 CHANGE IN RATE OF ADVANCE CORPORATION TAX: GENERAL POINTS

The rate of ACT is fixed for each financial year – that is to say, for each period starting on 1 April and ending on the following 31 March. Changes in the rate of ACT as between one financial year and the next give rise to a need for special rules about dividends paid in the period 1–5 April inclusive. The need for special rules is demonstrated by Example 23.

Example 23
Walkers Ltd pays a dividend of £21,000 on 3 April 1988. The relative rates of ACT and basic rates of income tax are as follows:

	ACT	*IT* (*basic rate*)
FY 1987	27/73	1987/88 27%
FY 1988	1/3	1988/89 25%

The dividend paid on 3 April 1988 is paid in the financial year 1988 which begins on 1 April 1988. If there were no provisions to the contrary, the ACT payable would be as follows:

£21,000 × 1/3 (rate for FY 1988) = £7,000

The amount taxable in the hands of shareholders is the total of the dividend and the tax credit:

	£
Dividend	21,000
Tax credit	7,000
Income	28,000

Basic rate tax on this amount of income for 1987/88 is 27%, i.e.:

£28,000 × 27% = £7,560

The amount of the tax credit available to shareholders is £7,000 while the basic rate tax liability on the income is £7,560.

While there is no theoretical reason why the tax credit should not differ from the basic rate liability on the income, since the introduction of the imputation system of corporation tax the functional relationships between basic rate income tax, tax credit and ACT have always been maintained. For dividends paid between 1 and 5 April inclusive, S.246(6), TA 1988 thus provides that the ACT rate applicable is to be the rate in force in the preceding financial year, and not the rate in force in the financial year in which the dividend is paid. In Example 23, above ACT paid in respect of the dividend on 3 April 1988 would thus be at the rate in force for FY 1987 – i.e., 27/73 – and not the rate in force for FY 1988 – 1/3. In this way, the tax credit or ACT equals the basic rate of income tax of 27% on the amount of the shareholder's income.

Special provisions in S.246(6)(b), TA 1988 apply to years in which there is a change in the rate of ACT.

Where a distribution is made on or before 5 April, and later in the same AP the company makes another distribution or receives FII, the period up to and including 5 April and the period after 5 April will be treated as separate APs for the purposes of determining ACT liabilities and the amount of any FII surpluses.

Example 24
Dancers Ltd prepares accounts for the 12 months ended 30 September 1988. On 10 February 1988, the company pays a dividend of £7,300. On 17 July 1988, it receives a dividend of £5,700. For the purposes of calculating ACT liability, Dancers Ltd will be treated as having two separate APs:
(a) the period 1 October 1987 to 5 April 1988; and
(b) the period 6 April 1988 to 30 September 1988.

In the first AP ((a)), the company pays a dividend of £7,300 and accounts for ACT of £7,300 × 27/73 = £2,700, giving a franked payment of £10,000.
In the second AP ((b)), the company receives a dividend of £5,700 which together with the tax credit of £1,900 (i.e., £5,700 × 1/3) amounts to FII of £7,600.
Normally the company would set off the FII against the franked payment, but that is not possible in this case because the FII is deemed to have arisen in a separate, later, AP.
It will be recalled that surplus FII may be carried forward to subsequent APs, but may not be carried back. Assuming no further distributions are made, and no FII received in the period ended 30 September 1988, the company will have paid ACT of £2,700 and at 30 September 1988 will have a surplus of FII of £7,600.

The introduction of a notional AP ending on 5 April applies solely for the purposes of calculating the company's ACT liability and surplus FII amounts. All other corporation tax computations will be carried out with reference to the company's *actual* AP, in accordance with the normal rules.

Question 3

Vibrations Ltd was incorporated in 1976, and trades as suppliers of musical instruments. It has no associated companies. During the accounting period ended 31 March 1988 the following transactions took place:

		£
10 April 1987	Dividend received on Beaters Ltd ordinary shares	1,460
1 July 1987	Paid half-year's dividend on £73,000 15% preference shares	5,475
11 July 1987	Made second payment under deed of covenant to the Rock Musicians Charity	730 (net)
10 October 1987	Received dividend on Electric Bongos Ltd ordinary shares	3,285
1 January 1988	Paid second half-year's dividend on preference shares	5,475
22 February 1988	Paid dividend on ordinary shares for the year ended 31 March 1987	29,200

Required:
Calculate the liability, if any, of Vibrations Ltd under Sched.13, TA 1988.

CHAPTER 4

THE COMPUTATION AND USE OF LOSSES

4.1 INTRODUCTION

This chapter will deal primarily with trading losses, although there will also be reference to certain other kinds of losses and deficits.

A trading loss is computed for corporation tax purposes in the same way as a trading profit (S.393(7), TA 1988). This means that capital allowances, which are deducted in arriving at a Schedule D Case I profit in the same way as any other trade expenses, may increase the amount of a trading loss, or alternatively may turn a trading profit into a loss.

> **Example 1**
> Consider a simple example of a company which has a trading profit of £100,000 and capital allowances of £120,000.
> The trading loss available for relief will be:
>
> | | £ |
> |---|---:|
> | Profit | 100,000 |
> | *Less*: Capital allowances | |
> | deducted as a trading expense | (120,000) |
> | | |
> | Trading loss | (20,000) |

A trading loss for corporation tax may be relieved in a number of alternative ways. It is the existence of alternatives which sometimes gives the question of loss relief the appearance of being difficult. In practice, however, the appropriate route is often clear.

4.2 CARRY FORWARD OF TRADING LOSSES

S.393(1), TA 1988 provides for the carry forward of the trading loss of an AP against *trading income* from the same trade in subsequent APs. The carry forward must be claimed within 6 years of the end of the AP in which the loss was incurred; however in practice a corporation tax computation showing a loss carried forward constitutes a claim.

Example 2
Allegro Ltd has the following results for the APs ended on the dates indicated. The facts given below will be used to illustrate the three most common types of loss relief.

Year ended	31 March 1987 (£)	31 March 1988 (£)	31 March 1989 (£)
Schedule D Case I profit/(loss)	20,000	(100,000)	65,000
Schedule A	16,000	20,000	22,000
Chargeable gain	4,000	5,000	1,000

Corporation tax computations

AP ended 31 March 1988

	£
Schedule D Case I	Nil
Schedule A	20,000
Chargeable gain	5,000
	25,000
Trading loss carried forward (S.393(1))	100,000

AP ended 31 March 1989

	£	£
Schedule D Case I	65,000	
Less: Loss brought forward S.393(1)	65,000	Nil
Schedule A		22,000
Chargeable gain		1,000
Profits chargeable to corporation tax		23,000

There are a number of points which should be noted about this computation:

(a) At this stage we are thinking only in terms of the carry forward of the loss. Other types of loss relief have been ignored.
(b) Note that since the company has income from sources other than its trade there is still a liability to corporation tax for these two APs.

(c) Lastly, and most important, note that a loss carried forward under S.393(1), TA 1988 may be set only against the *trading income*, that is to say the Schedule D Case I profits, of subsequent years. The loss position for carry forward to 1990 and subsequent years is thus as follows:

	£
Loss incurred in year ended 31 March 1988	100,000
Less: Utilised in year ended 31 March 1989	65,000
Loss to carry forward to 1990 and subsequent years	35,000

The carry forward of a trading loss is likely to be less attractive to a company than the loss reliefs that we will consider below. This is because the reliefs dealt with in 4.3 and 4.4 below will either reduce the amount of corporation tax payable in respect of the AP in which the loss arises, or will result in a repayment of corporation tax in respect of an earlier AP. However the possibility of the carry forward of a trading loss is still relevant to the extent that it is not possible to obtain relief in the AP of loss or in prior APs.

4.3   LOSS SET-OFF AGAINST OTHER PROFITS OF SAME ACCOUNTING PERIOD

We have seen in Example 2 that while the loss arising in the year ended 31 March 1988 was carried forward, the company's other income and chargeable gains remained liable to corporation tax.

S.393(2), TA 1988 gives a company the alternative possibility of claiming to set off a trading loss arising in an AP against the *total profits* of that same AP. You will recall that total profits comprise all the company's income *plus* its chargeable gains before deducting charges. The company may thus set a trading loss against a profit arising on a capital asset. However, although it is possible in this way to set off a trading loss against a capital profit, *the reverse is not true* – that is to say, it is not possible to set off a capital loss against a trading profit.

The time limit for making an election under S.393(2) is 2 years from the end of the AP in which the loss is incurred. In practice, the Inspector of Taxes will accept the making of the appropriate deductions in a computation as constituting a claim.

Example 3
Assume the same figures for Allegro Ltd as were given in Example 2, but now apply S.393(2) relief as outlined above.

Corporation Tax computations

AP ended 31 March 1988	£
Schedule D Case I	Nil
Schedule A	20,000
Chargeable gain	5,000
	25,000
Less: Loss relief S.393(2)	25,000
Profits chargeable to corporation tax	Nil

Summary:

	£
Loss incurred in year ended 31 March 1988	100,000
Less: Utilised in current year	25,000
	75,000
Balance of loss	75,000

Allegro Ltd at this stage can claim to carry forward the balance of the loss to the year ended 31 March 1989 under S.393(1), and if a claim is made the computation proceeds as follows:

AP ended 31 March 1989	£	£
Schedule D Case I	65,000	
Less: Loss brought forward (S.393(1))	65,000	Nil
Schedule A		22,000
Chargeable gain		1,000
Profits chargeable to corporation tax		23,000

Note that S.393(2) permits the loss to be set off against total profits but S.393(1) only permits the loss to be set off against Schedule D Case I profits in future years.

In this example, the loss has been used as follows:

	£
Loss arising in year ended 31 March 1988	100,000
Less: Utilised in year ended 31 March 1988	25,000
	75,000
Less: Utilised in year ended 31 March 1989	65,000
Balance of loss available to carry forward to subsequent year (S.393(1))	10,000

We have seen in Example 3 above that the loss was used first of all in the AP in which it arose under S.393(2), and thereafter the balance was carried forward under S.393(1). There is one further important possibility open to the company. Instead of carrying the balance of the loss forward at this stage it may claim to carry the balance of the loss *back*, and set it off against total profits of previous APs. If after having done that there still remains a balance of loss unrelieved it can be carried forward under S.393(1).

4.4   LOSS SET-OFF AGAINST PROFITS OF PREVIOUS ACCOUNTING PERIODS

The wording of S.393(2), TA 1988 offers the company a *two-stage relief*.
Here is what the section says:

> Where in any accounting period a company carrying on a trade incurs a loss in the trade, then . . . the company may make a claim requiring that the loss be set off for the purposes of corporation tax against profits (of whatever description) of that accounting period and, if the company was then carrying on the trade and the claim so requires, of preceding accounting periods ending within the time specified in Subsection (3). The 'claim so requires' means that the company makes such a claim.

The wording of this section makes it clear that relief is to be taken, *first* against the profits of the current AP, and *second* against the profits of the preceding AP.

A claim is competent for either the first stage of the relief only, or for both the first and second stages of the relief.

Period of carry back
The period of time for which a loss may be carried back is specified in S.393(3) and (4), TA 1988. In some cases, the amount of the profits against which the loss may be set will be restricted by reference to the length of the AP in which the loss is incurred. Most APs are 12 months long and in such cases the loss will be carried back and set off against the company's total profits for the 12 month AP preceding the 12 month in which the loss arose.

Example 4

Again we will assume the same figures for Allegro Ltd as were given in Example 2.

Corporation Tax computations

AP ended 31 March 1988	£
Schedule D Case I	Nil
Schedule A	20,000
Chargeable gain	5,000
	25,000
Less: Loss relief S.393(2)	25,000
Profits chargeable to corporation tax	Nil

Summary

Loss available for relief	100,000
Less: Utilised in year to 31 March 1988	25,000
Balance of loss available to carry back if required	75,000

AP ended 31 March 1987	£
Schedule D Case I	20,000
Schedule A	16,000
Chargeable gain	4,000
	40,000
Less: Loss carried back S.393(2)	40,000
Profits chargeable to corporation tax	Nil

Summary of loss relief	£	£
Loss available		100,000
Less: Utilised in year to 31 March 1988	25,000	
Utilised in year to 31 March 1987	40,000	
		65,000
Balance of loss which will be carried forward (S.393(1))		35,000

We have seen in Chapter 2 that companies which incurred capital expenditure prior to 1 April 1986 were entitled to FYAs. Such allowances were treated in the same way as any trade expense, and therefore could give rise to a trading loss. The legislation provided that in so far as a trading loss. The legislation provided that in so far as a trading loss was attributable wholly or partly to FYAs, the period of carry back under S.393(2) was extended from a maximum of 12 months to a maximum of 3 years.

Summary

The three alternative loss reliefs provided in S.393, TA 1988 may be summarised as follows:

A trading loss for an AP may be:

   (a) carried forward and set off against future trading profits, with no part of the loss being set off against total profits of the AP, *or*

   (b) set off against total profits of the AP, with any balance of loss then remaining being carried forward and set off against future trading profits as in (a) above, *or*

   (c) set off against total profits of the AP and then against total profits of the preceding AP, with any balance of loss then remaining being carried forward for set off against future trading profits, as in (a).

Of these alternatives (c) is the most common and in the case of a single company (i.e., one which is not a member of a group of companies) such as Allegro Ltd, offers relief at the earliest possible time with repayment of corporation tax and the possibility of a repayment supplement. In practice, the question of which relief or combination of reliefs is most advantageous for a given company will depend on the circumstances of that company.

There is one situation where the period of carry-back of a loss under S.393(2), TA 1988 differs from the general rule that we have so far considered.

4.4.1 Loss arising in accounting period of less than 12 months

When the loss arises in a 12 month AP the loss may be carried back and set off against the profits of the preceding 12 month AP. Where, however, the loss arises in an AP of less than 12 months the amount of the relief may be *restricted*. The profits of preceding APs which are available for relief are those earned in a period of time equal in length to the AP in which the loss is experienced. If a loss arises in an AP of 9 months the loss may thus be set off only against the profits for the 9 months preceding the AP in which the loss arose. The total profits of a preceding 9 month period will be arrived at by apportioning profits on a time basis.

Example 5
The results of Poco Ltd are as given below:

	Year ended 31 March 1988 (£)	9 months 31 December 1988 (£)	Year ended 31 December 1989 (£)
Schedule D Case I profit/(loss)	32,000	(60,000)	80,000
Schedule A	6,000	2,000	8,000
Chargeable gain	2,000	14,000	—

The possibility of group relief for the trading loss (see Chapter 5) is ignored in this example.
Poco Ltd has claimed loss relief under S.393, TA 1988 against profits of both the 9 month AP ended 31 December 1988 and part of the preceding AP of 12 months ended 31 March 1988.

Corporation tax computations

AP 1 April 1988 – 31 December 1988	£
Schedule D Case I	Nil
Schedule A	2,000
Chargeable gain	14,000
	16,000
Less: Loss relief S.393(2)	16,000
	Nil

Summary

Loss available for relief	60,000
Less: Utilised in current period	16,000
Loss available to carry back (but note that loss arises in 9 month AP).	44,000

AP 1 April 1987 – 31 March 1988
The loss of £60,000 arose in a 9 month AP. The balance of the loss, £44,000, may therefore be set only against computed profits for 9 months of the preceding 12 month AP. The computation proceeds as follows:

	£
Schedule D Case I	32,000
Schedule A	6,000
Chargeable gain	2,000
Total profits	40,000

less: S.393(2) relief
Profits for 12 months = £40,000
∴ profit for 9 months = £40,000 × 9/12 =
   £30,000
∴ maximum loss relief that may be

	£
claimed =	30,000
Profits chargeable to corporation tax	10,000

Summary

	£	£
Loss arising in 9 months to 31 December 1988		60,000
Less: Utilised in current period (S.393(2))	16,000	
Utilised against part of previous year's profits	30,000	46,000
Balance to carry forward (S.393(1))		14,000

4.4.2 Interaction between loss reliefs and charges

Loss relief claimed under S.393(2) is deducted from total profits and is deducted *before* charges. It is not possible to restrict the amount of loss relief claimed so as to leave sufficient profits to relieve the charges available. If a claim is made under S.393(2) the loss will be set off to the *maximum extent possible*, so as to exhaust the relevant total profits.

The situation will therefore arise in practice where the claiming of S.393(2) relief results in an excess of charges. You will remember that an 'excess of charges' means the amount by which charges exceed total profits. We have already seen that in so far as the excess of charges are 'trade charges', then that excess may be carried forward to future years (note that the excess *may not in any circumstances be carried back*) (S.393(9), TA 1988). Where, however, the charges are *not* trade charges they may not be carried forward, and the company does not obtain relief for them.

112 *Corporation tax*

Example 6

Lento Ltd makes up its accounts to 31 August each year. The following are its results for the years stated:

Years ended	31 August 1987 (£)	31 August 1988 (£)	31 August 1989 (£)
Schedule D Case I profit/(loss)	20,000	(55,000)	35,000
Schedule A	6,000	3,000	15,000
Chargeable gain	10,500	—	—
Charges on income:			
trade	12,000	12,000	12,000
non-trade	200	200	200

Lento Ltd claims loss relief under S.393(2), TA 1988 for both the AP of loss and the preceding AP.

Corporation tax computations:

AP ended 31 August 1988	£
Schedule D Case I	Nil
Schedule A	3,000
	3,000
Less: Loss relief (S.393(2))	3,000
	Nil

The charges are £12,200, and since after application of loss relief there are no profits against which they can be relieved there are excess charges of £12,200. The trade charges, £12,000, may be carried forward as a trading expense (S.393(9), TA 1988). The non-trade charges, £200, may not be carried forward.

AP ended 31 August 1987	£
Schedule D Case I	20,000
Schedule A	6,000
Chargeable gain	10,500
	36,500
Less: Loss relief (S.393(2))	36,500
Profits chargeable to corporation tax	Nil

Excess charges available to carry forward from the AP ended 31 August 1987 are £12,000. Note again that the company will not obtain relief for the non-trade charges of £200.

Summary of loss relief	£	£
Loss available for relief		55,000
Less: Loss utilised 1988	3,000	
1987	36,500	39,500

	£
Loss available to carry forward to (S.393(1))	15,500

The loss carried forward of £15,500 is aggregated with the trade charges carried forward under S.393(9) so that the total amount of loss relief and trade charges available to deduct from the Schedule D Case I profit for the year ended 31 August 1989 is:

	£
Loss available to carry forward	15,500
Trade charges carried forward from the year ended 31 August 1987	12,000
Trade charges carried forward from the year ended 31 August 1988	12,000
Total	39,500

AP ended 31 August 1989	£	£
Schedule D Case I	35,000	
Less: Loss and trade charges brought forward (S.393(1) and S.393(9))	39,500	Nil
Schedule A		15,000
		15,000
Less: Charges (current AP)		12,200
Profits chargeable to corporation tax		2,800

Losses and trade charges brought forward under S.393(1) and S.393(9) may be deducted only from Schedule D Case I profits. The amount to be carried forward to later years is thus as follows:

	£
Loss and trade charges brought forward	39,500
Less: Utilised year ended 31 August 1989	35,000
Carried forward to 1990 and subsequent years	4,500

It has been pointed out that as a result of claiming relief under S.393(2) for the year of loss and the preceding year, the company loses the benefit of relief for non-trade charges. Non-trade charges, as the name suggests, have about them the notion of 'gratuity', such as a 4 year deed of covenant to a charity. It follows that in most companies they are unlikely to be so large in amount that they will be a determining factor in whether or not to claim S.393(2) relief. If, exceptionally, the loss of relief is significant a

company would consider carrying forward a trading loss, o
restricting a S.393(2) claim to the year of loss.

4.5 TERMINAL LOSS RELIEF

If a company experiences a trading loss in the last 12 months of
carrying on its trade, it can set off the loss against income from the
trade arising in the 3 years preceding the final year of trading. To
arrive at the trading loss of the final 12 months and the trading
income of the preceding 3 years, apportionments are made, as
necessary, on a time basis.

The terminal loss may also include an excess of charges over
total profits in the final 12 month period of trading. In this case the
excess charges will be restricted (as for the carry forward of trading
losses) to the amount of trade charges.

Terminal loss relief is an exception to the general principle that
a trading loss carried back is set against total profits. Relief is
restricted to set-off against the Schedule D Case I profits of the 3
years preceding the final 12 months of trading, starting with the
latest year first.

Terminal loss relief is given only after all other loss reliefs which
may be available have been applied. Relief must thus be taken
under S.393(2) *before* applying terminal loss relief.

The final point to be noted in connection with the application of
terminal loss relief is that this relief may not interfere with relief
for charges paid wholly and exclusively for the purposes of the
trade (S.393(5), TA 1988). The effect of this rule is that trade
charges must be relieved before terminal loss relief is given. In a
simple computation where the company has no sources of income
other than Schedule D Case I profits, the trade charges will
therefore be deducted from the trading profits first and then the
terminal loss relief will be given. Where the company has other
profits in addition to trading profits, the trade charges will be dealt
with as follows:

(a) set off trade charges against profits other than trading
profits,

(b) set off balance of trade charges against Schedule D Case
I profits, and

(c) finally set off terminal loss relief against trading profits.

The rule which 'protects' trade charges is a common-sense approach to the juxtaposition of the two reliefs, for trade charges and for the terminal loss. It would not make sense to grant relief for a terminal loss if this gave rise to an equal loss of relief in respect of charges. Where there is a loss of relief for trade charges in the context of S.393(2) (set-off of trading loss against total profits of current and preceding APs), the excess trade charges are carried forward as trading expenses to future APs. Such an option is not practicable in the case of a ceasing trade.

Example 7

Failure Ltd made up accounts to 31 March each year. The company ceased trading on 31 March 1989. The results for the 4 years prior to cessation are as follows:

Year ended	1986 (£)	1987 (£)	1988 (£)	1989 (£)
Schedule D Case I profit/(loss)	11,000	12,500	1,000	(23,000)
UFII	400	500	500	500
Trade charges	1,300	1,300	1,400	1,000

The company claims terminal loss relief under S.394, TA 1988.

(1) *Application of S.393(2), TA 1988*

AP ended 31 March 1989	£
Schedule D Case I	Nil
UFII	500
	500
Less: Loss relief (S.393(2))	500
Profits chargeable to corporation tax	Nil

AP ended 31 March 1988	£
Schedule D Case I profit	1,000
UFII	500
	1,500
Less: Loss relief (S.393.2))	1,500
Profits chargeable to corporation tax	Nil

Note that we are left with charges unutilised of £1,400 for the year ended 31 March 1988 and £1,000 for the year ended 31 March 1989.

The charges for the final year will be included in the computation of the terminal loss since they are all trade charges. The charges of £1,400 for the year ended 31 March 1988 may not be included in the terminal loss computation (because they do not arise in the final 12 months of trading) and will thus not be relieved.

(2) *Calculation of terminal loss*

	£	£
Loss for year ended 31 March 1989		23,000
Less: Utilised under S.393(2)		
Year ended 31 March 1989	500	
Year ended 31 March 1988	1,500	2,000
		21,000
Add: Trade charges for final 12 months		1,000
		22,000
Terminal loss		

(3) *Calculation of profits available for terminal loss relief*

AP ended 31 March 1988	£
Profits available for terminal loss relief	Nil

AP ended 31 March 1987	£
Trade charges which must be protected:	
Trade charges	1,300
Less: Set-off against UFII	500
Trade charges which are deducted from trading profits before application of terminal loss relief	800

Therefore profits available for terminal loss relief:

	£
Schedule D Case I	12,500
Less: Trade charges 'protected'	800
Profits available for terminal loss relief	11,700

AP ended 31 March 1986	£
Trade charges which must be protected:	
Trade charges	1,300
Less: Set-off against UFII	400
Trade charges which must be deducted from trading profits before application of terminal loss relief	900

Therefore profits available for terminal loss relief:

	£
Schedule D Case I	11,000
Less: Trade charges protected	900
Profits available for terminal loss relief	10,100

(4) *Application of terminal loss relief*

AP ended 31 March 1987	£	£
Schedule D Case I	12,500	
Less: Terminal loss relief	11,700	
		800
UFII		500
		1,300
Less: Charges		1,300
Profits chargeable to corporation tax		Nil

AP ended 31 March 1986	£	£
Schedule D Case I	11,000	
Less: Terminal loss relief	10,100	
		900
UFII		400
		1,300
Less: Charges		1,300
Profits chargeable to corporation tax		Nil

Summary	£	£
Terminal loss relief available		22,000
Less: Utilised		
Year ended 31 March 1987	11,700	
Year ended 31 March 1986	10,100	21,800
Balance of terminal loss relief not utilised		200

In Example 7 the final AP was 12 months in length and therefore the computations were relatively simple. In Example 8 the final AP is less than 12 months long. It will be seen that, in order to arrive at the terminal loss of the final 12 months and the trading income of the preceding 3 years, a number of apportionments are necessary.

Example 8

Complete Failure Ltd ceases trading on 31 March 1989. The following are the results for the year stated and for the final 3 months of trading:

Years ended 31 December

	1985 (£)	1986 (£)	1987 (£)	1988 (£)	3 months ended 31 March 1989 (£)
Schedule D Case I profit/(loss)	5,000	10,000	8,000	4,000	(50,000)
Schedule A	2,000	2,000	1,000	2,000	1,000
Charges: trade	1,500	1,500	1,500	1,500	375
non-trade	—	—	—	500	125

The company claims terminal loss relief under S.394, TA 1988.

(1) *Application of S.393(2)*

AP 3 months ended 31 March 1989	£
Schedule D Case I	Nil
Schedule A	1,000
	1,000
Less: Loss relief (S.393(2))	1,000
Profits chargeable to corporation tax	Nil

Year ended 31 December 1988	£
Schedule D Case I	4,000
Schedule A	2,000
	6,000
Less: Loss relief (S.393(2)) *(Note: Loss arose in a 3 month AP and can therefore be set only against profits of 3 months to 31 December 1988)* ∴ relief restricted to £6,000 × 3/12 =	1,500
	4,500
Less: Charges	2,000
Profits chargeable to corporation tax (before terminal loss relief)	2,500

(2) *Calculation of terminal loss available for relief*

	£	£
Trading loss for final 3 months		50,000
Trading loss for previous 9 months – profit ∴		Nil
		50,000
Less: Relief given under S.393(2)		
AP ended 31 March 1987	1,000	
AP ended 31 December 1988	1,500	2,500
		47,500

Add: Excess charges for
AP of 3 months
ended 31 March 1989   375

Terminal loss   47,875

(3) *Calculation of trading profits available for terminal loss relief*
Two points should be noted:
(a) The terminal loss relief may be set only against trading profits for
     the 3 years preceding the final 12 months – i.e., profits for the
     period 1 April 1985 to 31 March 1988.
(b) As in Example 7, you have to make sure that the giving of
     terminal loss relief does not interfere with relief for trade
     charges:

		Trading profits available for relief (£)	(£)	Period
(i)	Period of 3 months ended 31 March 1988 $3/12 \times £4,000$		1,000	3 months
(ii)	Year ended 31 December 1987 *Less*: Trade charges 'protected'	8,000 500	7,500	1 year
(iii)	Year ended 31 December 1986		10,000	1 year
(iv)	Period of 9 months from 1 April 1985 to 31 December 1985 $9/12 \times £5,000$		3,750	9 months
			22,250	3 years

(4) *Application of terminal loss relief*

AP ended 31 December 1988	£	
Schedule D Case I profit	4,000	
Less: Terminal loss relief	1,000	3,000
Schedule A		2,000
		5,000
Less: Loss relief (S.393(2))		1,500
		3,500
Less: Charges		2,000
Profits chargeable to corporation tax		1,500

AP ended 31 December 1987	£	£
Schedule D Case I profits	8,000	
Less: Terminal loss relief	7,500	500
Schedule A		1,000
		1,500
Less: Charges		1,500
Profits chargeable to corporation tax		Nil

AP ended 31 December 1986	£	£
Schedule D Case I profits	10,000	
Less: Terminal loss relief	10,000	Nil
Schedule A		2,000
		2,000
Less: Charges		1,500
Profits chargeable to corporation tax		500

AP ended 31 December 1985	£	£
Schedule D Case I profits	5,000	
Less: Terminal loss relief	3,750	1,250
Schedule A		2,000
		3,250
Less: Charges		1,500
Profits chargeable to corporation tax		1,750

Summary	
Terminal loss relief available	47,875
Less: Utilised	22,250
Balance of terminal loss unrelieved	25,625

4.6 SET-OFF OF TRADING LOSSES AND OTHER ITEMS AGAINST SURPLUS FRANKED INVESTMENT INCOME

We have seen in Chapter 1 that FII is not brought into the computation of profits chargeable to corporation tax. The main use of FII is the set-off against franked payments made during an AP since the company is liable to pay ACT only in respect of the

excess of franked payments made over FII received. Full use of th
company's FII can be made only if the franked payments equal c
exceed the amount of the dividends received plus the attached ta
credit.

If, however, an investment or other company receives FII whic
exceeds in total the amount of its franked payments in the AP th
company will have what is called a *surplus of FII*. This will b
carried forward to the next AP and will be regarded as F1
received by the company in that period (S.241(3), TA 1988
Where, however, the company makes a claim under S.242, T/
1988, the surplus FII of the AP, excluding surpluses brougl
forward, will be treated as if it were an additional amount c
profits chargeable to corporation tax. The company may then se
off against these deemed 'profits' several types of losses an
expenses including:

> (a) trading losses available for relief under S.393(2), T/
>   1988 but which cannot be relieved against total profit
>   because profits are insufficient,
> (b) charges – both trade charges and other charges.

Before going on to look at the relief in detail, we should perhap
explain that the relief (in the shape of a repayment of the tax credi
inherent in FII) is unlike other loss reliefs in that some time afte
the repayment has been received it may become necessary i
certain circumstances to *repay the cash received back to the Inlan*
Revenue. The more usual loss reliefs give a permanent reduction ii
profits with, perhaps, a repayment of tax, which one is never calle
upon to pay back. In contrast, this relief is a 'cash flow' relief
which is to a greater or lesser extent (depending on circumstances
a *temporary relief*. When the amount of the relief is repaid to th
Revenue, the company is put back in the position in which it founc
itself before the claim for relief was made.

If in an AP a company has a surplus of FII and, let us say, a
trading loss, and relief for the whole of the trading loss has no
proved possible under S.393(2) (set-off against total profits) ther
the surplus of FII is treated as additional profits, and the tax credi
inherent in the income is repaid.

Example 9
Commotions Ltd has the following results for its AP ended 31 Marcl
1989:

	£
Schedule D Case I Loss	(28,000)
FII	25,000
Franked payments made	15,000

The company claims relief under S.242, TA 1988:

S.242 Claim

Surplus FII treated as profits	10,000
Less: Trading loss	28,000
Balance of loss carried forward (S.393(1))	18,000
Tax credit repayment £10,000 at 25% =	2,500

The trading losses which may be utilised in a S.242 claim are losses which are available for relief under S.393(2), TA 1988 but which have not been utilised because of an absence of normal profits chargeable to corporation tax (S.242(3), TA 1988). It is significant that S.393(2) is referred to, for you will recollect that loss relief under that section is given in *two stages*, first against other profits of the AP of loss and then against total profits of the preceding AP. A loss arising for example in the 12 month AP ended 31 August 1988 may thus be set firstly against surplus FII of that AP, and secondly against surplus FII, if any, of the AP ending 31 August 1987.

We have seen in this chapter and in Chapter 3 that a surplus of FII is, in the absence of a S.242 claim, carried forward and treated as FII received in the subsequent period. It is important to note, however, that when considering S.242 relief, any surplus of FII brought forward from earlier APs is left out of account. It is only the surplus arising within the AP with which we are concerned.

Claims for relief under S.242 are made within 2 years of the AP of loss in the case of a claim for a trading loss. In the case of excess charges, the time limit is 6 years from the end of the AP in which the charges were paid.

Example 10
Promotions Ltd has the following results for its 12 month AP ended 31 March 1988.

	£
Schedule D Case I Loss	(50,000)
Schedule A	6,500
FII received in year to 31 March 1988	81,000

Franked payments made	25,000
Surplus FII brought forward from year to 31 March 1987	10,000

Promotions Ltd claims relief under SS.393(2) and 242, TA 1988:

(a) *Claims under S.393(2), TA 1988*

	£
Schedule D Case I	Nil
Schedule A	6,500
Less: Loss relief (S.393(2))	6,500
Profits chargeable to corporation tax	Nil

Summary

Loss available	50,000
Less: Loss relieved (S.393(2))	6,500
Loss still available	43,500

(b) *Claim under S.242, TA 1988*

Surplus of FII in current year	56,000
Less: Loss relief (S.242)	43,500
Balance of surplus FII of current year	12,500
Add: Surplus of FII of previous year	10,000
Surplus FII carried forward to year to 31 March 1989	22,500

Tax credit repayment
£43,500 × 25% = £10,875

Summary

	£	£
Trading loss available		50,000
Less: Used S.393(2)	6,500	
Used S.242	43,500	50,000
Balance of loss		Nil

4.7 EFFECT OF S.242 CLAIM IN SUBSEQUENT YEARS

You will note in Example 10 that as a result of making a S.242 claim:

(a) There is no loss relief available to carry forward to subsequent years.

(b) The surplus FII available to carry forward to subsequent years is £22,500. (If no S.242 claim had been made, the surplus FII carried forward would have been £66,000.)

f, in a subsequent AP, the franked payments made by Promotions .td exceed the FII, the company will have to account for a larger mount of ACT than would have been payable if no S.242 claim ad previously been made. This is because the amount of surplus 'II available to set off against the franked payments is £22,500, vhereas if no S.242 claim had been made the amount available for et-off would have been £66,000.

Example 11
In its AP ended 31 March 1989 Promotions Ltd receives FII of £18,000 and makes franked payments of £90,000. The ACT payable is calculated as follows:

Advance corporation tax accounting

	£	£
Franked payments		90,000
Less: Surplus FII brought forward	22,500	
FII received in year ended 31 March 1989	18,000	40,500
Excess of franked payments over FII		49,500

ACT payable:
£49,500 × 25% = £12,375

If the company had not made a S.242 claim in 1988, the ACT payable in respect of the year ended 31 March 1989 would have been calculated as follows:

	£	£
Franked payments		90,000
Less: Surplus FII brought forward	66,000	
FII of current year	18,000	84,000
Excess of franked payments over FII		6,000

ACT payable:
£6,000 × 25% = £1,500

Where franked payments exceed FII in an AP subsequent to a S.242 claim in an earlier AP, as in Example 11 above, two legislative mechanisms are applied which, as mentioned above have the effect of putting the company back in the position it had before the S.242 claim was made. This means that the S.242 payment to the company is repaid to the Revenue (by an indirect route), and the loss applied against the surplus FII in the course of the claim is restored to the company. The legislative provisions are as follows:

(a) The amount of ACT which may be deducted from the corporation tax liability is restricted to the amount actually paid *less* the amount of the tax credit repaid to the company previously on making a S.242 claim (S.244(2), TA 1988). The indirect effect of this is to repay to the Revenue the tax credit repayment to the company by increasing the amount of mainstream corporation tax by the same amount.

Example 12
In Example 11, Promotions Ltd paid ACT of £12,375 in the year ended 31 March 1989.
The ACT which may be deducted from corporation tax payable in respect of the year ended 31 March 1989 is:

	£
ACT paid	12,375
Less: Tax credit repayment in year ended 31 March 1988	11,745
Restricted ACT deductible from corporation tax liability	630

(b) The whole of the loss previously used against the surplus FII is restored to the company in the form of a trading loss brought forward (as for S.393(1), TA 1988) to the AP in which franked payments exceed FII (S.242(5), TA 1988).

Example 13
Assume that Promotions Ltd had the following results for its AP ended 31 March 1989:

	£
Schedule D Case I profit	120,000
Schedule A	1,200

The rate of CT is 35%

Corporation tax computation

AP ended 31 March 1989	£	£
Schedule D Case I	120,000	
Less: Loss restored (S.242(5))	43,500	76,500
Schedule A		1,200
Profits chargeable to corporation tax		77,700
Corporation tax payable:		
£77,700 × 35% =		27,195
Less: ACT (see Example 12)		630
Mainstream corporation tax		£26,565

4.8 OTHER LOSSES AND DEFICITS

Throughout this chapter, we have concentrated on relief available for trading losses, and we have seen how in certain circumstances it is possible to set trading losses against profits other than trading profits. Other kinds of deficits and allowable capital losses may be set off only against future surpluses or gains of the same nature.

Example 15
Mixed Emotions Ltd makes up accounts to 31 March each year and has the following results for the years stated:

Years ended	31 March 1988 (£)	31 March 1989 (£)
Schedule D Case I profit (loss)	50,000	(8,000)
UFII	2,000	2,500
Schedule A (deficit)/surplus	(200)	3,000
Chargeable gains/(allowable loss)	(600)	6,000

The company claims relief under S.393(2), TA 1988.

AP ended 31 March 1989	£	£
Schedule D Case I		Nil
UFII		2,500
Schedule A	3,000	
Less: Deficit brought forward	200	2,800

Chargeable gain	6,000	
Less: Allowable loss		
brought forward	600	5,400
		10,700
Less: Loss relief (S.393(2))		8,000
Profits chargeable to		
corporation tax		2,700

4.9   CONSEQUENCES OF LOSS CLAIMS

A trading loss relief claim will normally result in a repayment of corporation tax or the reduction or the elimination of a liability to corporation tax. Among other possible consequences are the following:

(1) A repayment of income tax if the profits of the AP in which the loss arises include UFII and the income tax suffered has not been relieved elsewhere – see Chapter 1.

(2) A reduction in the rate of corporation tax as a result of a fall in the level of the company's profits to within the small companies rate band or the marginal small companies rate band – see Chapter 1.

(3) The payment by the Inland Revenue of a 'repayment supplement' in certain cases where corporation tax or income tax is repaid to the company – see Chapter 1.

(4) The creation of a surplus of ACT and consequential changes in ACT computations if the loss relief reduces the income of the company so that the maximum ACT that may be deducted from the corporation tax payable is reduced – see Chapter 3.

(5) The reduction or elimination of a 'shortfall' in the context of a family 'close' company – see Chapter 6.

Question 4

Machinations Ltd has the following results:

Years ended 31 March	1986 (£)	1987 (£)	1988 (£)	1989 (£)
Trading profit/(loss)	16,000	3,200	(15,000)	22,400
Capital allowances	9,360	900	7,350	320
Debenture interest received (gross)	1,500	4,000	4,000	4,000
Rents received	720	720	720	720
Capital loss	(4,350)	—	—	—
Capital gain	—	—	5,600	—
Royalties paid (gross)	1,000	3,100	3,100	3,100
Covenant to SSPCA – Charity (gross)	500	500	500	500

Required:
Show the corporation tax payable and income tax repayable (if any) for each AP, assuming that relief is taken at the earliest opportunity.
Assume the following rates of tax:

	(%)
Corporation tax	35
Income tax	25

CHAPTER 5

GROUPS OF COMPANIES

5.1 THE NATURE OF A GROUP OF COMPANIES

The basic unit of charge to corporation tax is an *individual company*. For certain purposes, however, the corporation tax legislation looks beyond the separate company to companies associated with it in a group of companies. Sometimes taking account of companies in the group has the effect of restricting or limiting some relief or benefit – e.g., in the computation of the maximum relevant income of close companies (see Chapter 6) or in connection with the application of the small company rate of corporation tax (see Chapter 1). In other cases, the existence of a group makes it possible to obtain special reliefs and advantages.

There are four common kinds of advantages enjoyed by companies which are members of groups. These are:

(1) The setting-off of the trading losses of one group member against the profits of another (S.402 et seq., TA 1988) (see 5.2).

(2) The payment of dividends by a subsidiary to a parent company without accounting for ACT and payment of interest gross (i.e., without payment of income tax) by a subsidiary to a parent company (S.247 et seq., TA 1988) (see 5.3).

(3) The surrendering of ACT paid by a parent company to a subsidiary and treating the ACT surrendered as paid by the subsidiary (S.240, TA 1988) (see 5.4).

(4) The transfer of assets between members of the same group of companies without giving rise to capital gains chargeable to corporation tax (S.272 et seq., TA 1970).

The relevant group structures in each of the four situations above are different one from the other, but have many points of similarity.

Each group structure involves the notion of a *parent* and a *subsidiary* company. The more important relationships are where one company is a 51% subsidiary of another and where one company is a 75% subsidiary of another.

To say one company is a 51% subsidiary of another means that more than 50% of the ordinary share capital is owned by the other. In the same way, to describe a company as a 75% subsidiary means that at least 75% of the ordinary share capital is owned by the other (S.838(1), TA 1988). 'Ordinary share capital' means all the issued share capital of a company other than capital entitled to a fixed rate of dividend only – e.g., preference shares (S.832(1), TA 1988).

When determining the extent of the share ownership by one company in another it is necessary to consider both *direct* and *indirect* ownership. Where company A owns shares in company B and company B owns shares in company C then company A is said to have indirect ownership of shares in company C through company B.

Example 1

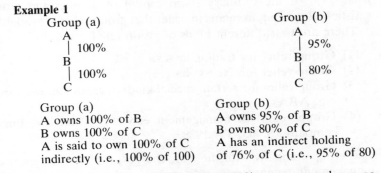

Group (a)
A owns 100% of B
B owns 100% of C
A is said to own 100% of C indirectly (i.e., 100% of 100)

Group (b)
A owns 95% of B
B owns 80% of C
A has an indirect holding of 76% of C (i.e., 95% of 80)

Both (a) and (b) are what are called *75% groups*, and are so described even if the actual share ownership (direct and indirect) is more than 75%. Relief for trading losses and 'tax free' transfers of assets arise in 75% structures ((1) and (4) above); surrender of ACT and special group dividends and payments of interest (2) and (3) above) arise in 51% structures.

5.2 GROUP RELIEF

Group relief is available between a parent and its 75% subsidiary and between two or more 75% subsidiaries of the same parent. In addition to meeting the definition of 75% subsidiary referred to above, group relief is available only where the parent in relation to the subsidiary is entitled to not less than 75% of the profits available for distribution to equity holders, and to not less than 75% of the subsidiary's assets available to equity holders on a notional winding up (S.413, TA 1988). An equity holder is defined in Sched.18, TA 1988 as a person holding ordinary shares or a loan creditor where the loan is not a normal commercial loan. These 1973 provisions comprised anti-avoidance legislation aimed at certain special share structures and arrangements which were developed in the years before 1973 to take advantage of features of the group structure for group relief purposes. In most straightforward commercial cases the parents of 75% subsidiaries (defined, as above, as companies whose ordinary share capital is held at least to the extent of 75% by their parents) will also be entitled to 75% of profits available to equity holders and to 75% of assets available on a winding-up to equity holders.

In what follows, it will be assumed that when a company owns at least 75% of the ordinary share capital of another the group satisfies all the requirements in order that group relief is available.

There are four different kinds of group relief:

(1) Group relief for trading losses.
(2) Group relief for excess charges.
(3) Group relief for certain special kinds of capital allowances –
    e.g. ABAs.
(4) Group relief for management expenses of an investment
    company (S.403, TA 1988).

The group company with the loss, charges, capital allowances or management expenses is said to surrender the loss or charge, etc. and is called the *surrendering company*. The company against whose profits the loss or charge is set is said to claim the loss, and is called the *claimant company*.

In each case, the items available in the surrendering company are set off against the claimant company's total profits for the *corresponding AP*. As between the group company surrendering the loss and a group claimant company, the amount of the loss which may be surrendered is subject to a maximum. The maximum which may be surrendered is the amount of the loss or the amount of the claimant company's chargeable profits, whichever is the less. In particular, there is no question of a company surrendering a loss in excess of the claimant's relevant profits and the claimant company then carrying forward or carrying back the excess of the losses surrendered. A claim for group relief must be made within 2 years of the end of the surrendering company's AP (S.412, TA 1988).

5.2.1 Group relief for trading losses

Group relief permits a company to set off a trading loss not only against its own profits in the ways we have seen in Chapter 4, but also against the total profits of companies in the same 75% group.

Example 2
Lord Ltd is a manufacturing company which makes up its accounts to 31 December in each year. Vassal Ltd is the wholly owned subsidiary of Lord Ltd and makes up its accounts to 31 December in each year also. The following are the results for the year ended 31 December 1988.

	Lord Ltd (£)	Vassall Ltd (£)
Schedule D Case I profit/(loss)	50,000	(270,000)
Schedule A surplus	7,500	
Chargeable gain	60,000	
UFII	12,000	10,000

The amount of trading loss available for group relief is £270,000. The amount which may be relieved is, however, limited to the profits available for relief as follows:

Total profits of Lord Ltd

	£
Schedule D Case I	50,000
Schedule A	7,500
UFII	12,000
Chargeable gain	60,000
Profits available for relief	129,500

The relief is applied in the corporation tax computation of Lord Ltd with the effect of reducing the profits chargeable in Lord Ltd to nil.

Lord Ltd
Corporation tax computation
AP ended 31 December 1988

	£
Schedule D Case I	50,000
Schedule A	7,500
UFII	12,000
Chargeable gain	60,000
Total profits and profits chargeable	129,500
Less: Group relief	129,500
	Nil

As stated above, the amount of trading loss available for group relief is £270,000. However in some cases the surrendering company will take as much relief for its trading loss as is possible against its own profits *before* seeking relief against the profits of a group member. In Example 2, Vassal Ltd might first set off £10,000 of its trading loss against its own profits of £10,000 (UFII) and, assuming chargeable profits for the year ended 31 December 1987 of £40,000, it could carry back £40,000 of loss under S.393(2). The loss available for group relief would then be £220,000, but since only £129,500 (i.e., the chargeable profits of the claimant company) may be surrendered, the balance of the loss (i.e., £90,500) will be carried forward and deducted from future trading profits of Vassal Ltd (S.393(1), TA 1988). The loss of Vassal Ltd would thus have been utilised as follows:

Vassal Ltd

	£	£
Schedule D Case I loss		270,000
Less: Utilised (S.393(2))		
AP ended 31/12/88	10,000	
AP ended 31/12/87	40,000	
		50,000
		220,000
Less: Surrendered to Lord Ltd		129,500
Loss carried forward (S.393(1))		90,500

5.2.2 Group relief for excess charges

A surrendering company may pass on to any other company in the same 75% group so much of its charges as exceed its profits. It

should however, be particularly noted that in this context the term
'profits' has a specific meaning given to it in S.403(8), TA 1988.
For these purposes, the 'profits' are arrived at *before* deducting
any losses or allowances which originated in some other AP. This
means that, for example, losses brought forward under S.393(1)
from an earlier AP must be *ignored* when deciding whether there
are any excess charges available to surrender. Likewise a loss
which could be carried back under S.393(2), TA 1988 to an earlier
AP must also be ignored when calculating group relief for excess
charges available for surrender in that earlier AP.

Example 3
Filius Ltd is the wholly owned subsidiary of Pater Ltd and has the
following results for the year ended 31 March 1988:

	£
Schedule D Case I profit	6,000
Schedule A surplus	1,000
Chargeable gains	500

In the year ended 31 March 1988 Filius Ltd paid debenture interest of
£12,000.
An excess of charges arises as follows:

AP ended 31 March 1988

	£
Schedule D Case I	6,000
Schedule A	1,000
Chargeable gain	500
Total profits	7,500
Less: Charges	12,000
Excess charges	4,500

The excess of charges, £4,500 is available for surrender by way of
group relief against the total profits arising in Pater Ltd for its
accounting year ended 31 March 1988.

Example 4
Minor Ltd is a wholly owned subsidiary of Major Ltd and has a
Schedule D Case I profit of £8,000 for the year ended 31 December
1988. Patent royalties of £10,000 were paid (gross) during this AP.
There are losses brought forward from earlier APs under S.393(1),
TA 1988 of £5,000.

The corporation tax computation will proceed as follows:

AP ended 31 December 1988

	£	£
Schedule D Case I profit		8,000
Less: Losses brought forward (S.393(1))		5,000
		3,000
Less: Charges:		
Patent royalties paid	10,000	
Less: Used year ending 31/12/88	3,000	3,000
Excess charges	7,000	
Profits chargeable to corporation tax		Nil

The excess charges of £7,000, being trade charges, may be carried forward (S.393(9)).

For group relief purposes, however, the excess charges will be calculated as follows:

	£
Schedule D Case I profit	8,000
Less: Charges	10,000
Excess charges for group relief	2,000

The excess of charges, £2,000 is available to surrender to Major Ltd under the group relief provisions for set off against its total profits for the accounting year ended 31 December 1988.

One of the fundamental principles of group relief is that losses, excess charges, etc. are available only to surrender from one group company to another in so far as they arise in a '*corresponding AP*'. A corresponding AP is defined by the legislation with reference to the company which has a loss, etc. to surrender. If an AP of a claimant company coincides with an AP of a surrendering company (in the sense of covering the same period of time) then the AP of the claimant company is said to 'correspond' with the AP of the surrendering company. In Example 4, Major and Minor thus both have APs of 12 months ended 31 December 1988 and the APs are corresponding periods. The principle that only excess charges of corresponding APs may be relieved is exemplified in Example 4 by the fact that if the S.393(1) loss of Minor Ltd had been deducted from the trading profits before deducting royalties the excess charges for group relief would have been £7,000 – i.e., £5,000 greater – and the company would have effectively been able to use the group relief provisions to surrender a loss arising in an earlier AP.

5.2.3 Corresponding accounting periods

In the examples so far considered, the APs of the surrendering company and the claimant company have coincided. The losses or excess charges have thus been available to deduct from the total profits of the claimant company, subject only to the limit of the amount of the profits of the claimant company or the amount of the loss, etc. of the surrendering company, whichever is the less.

Where, however, the claimant and the surrendering company do not have corresponding APs, it becomes necessary to *apportion* the profits of the claimant company, against which group relief may be set, and the loss or other type of relief available for surrender. This is done in order to ensure that relief is given only for that period of time which is common to the APs of both the surrendering and claimant companies.

Example 5
C Ltd and S Ltd are members of a 75% group. S Ltd incurred a trading loss of £100,000 in the year ended 31 December 1988. The APs and results of C Ltd are:

12 months to:	Profit (£)
31 March 1988	80,000
31 March 1989	120,000

Corresponding accounting periods are

(a) *Period 1 January 1988 to 31 March 1988*
The loss which may be surrendered by S Ltd is £100,000 × 3/12 = £25,000.
The profit of C Ltd against which the group relief may be set is £80,000 × 3/12 = £20,000.
S Ltd will surrender the smaller of these two figures (namely £20,000), and C Ltd may thus claim group relief of £20,000 to set against its profits of £80,000 for the period ended 31 March 1988.

(b) *Period 1 April 1988 to 31 December 1988*
The loss which may be surrendered by S Ltd is £100,000 × 9/12 = £75,000.
The profit of C Ltd against which the group relief may be set is £120,000 × 9/12 = £90,000.
S Ltd will surrender the smaller of these two figures (namely £75,000), and C Ltd may thus claim group relief of £75,000 against its profits for the year ended 31 March 1989.

It should be noted that the total loss surrendered by S Ltd is £95,000 (i.e., £20,000 + £75,000), thus there is a balance of loss of £5,000 which may not be surrendered under the group relief provisions. This must be dealt with under the normal loss relief provisions discussed in Chapter 4.

5.2.4 Companies joining or leaving group

The general rule is that group relief will not be available unless the surrendering company and claimant company are both members of the same group throughout the whole of their respective APs (S.409(1), TA 1988). However to give effect to the intention to give relief for the time companies are members of the same group, an AP is deemed to end, and a new AP to commence, whenever a company joins or leaves a group. The new AP then continues until the end of the actual AP. It should be stressed that this artificial splitting up of the companies' true APs is done solely for the purpose of ascertaining the amount of group relief available.

Example 6
A Ltd, a trading company, has 2 wholly owned subsidiaries, B Ltd and D Ltd. All 3 companies make up accounts to 31 December in each year. B Ltd has been a subsidiary of A Ltd for many years, but D Ltd became a subsidiary of A Ltd on 1 July 1988. The results of the 3 group members for the year ended 31 December 1988 are as follows:

	A Ltd (£)	B Ltd (£)	D Ltd (£)
Schedule D Case I profit/(loss)	280,000	50,000	(100,000)
Schedule A surplus	25,000		
Chargeable gain	14,000		

Assume A Ltd is the claimant company in relation to the surrendering company D Ltd. For the purposes of group relief the APs of A

Ltd and D Ltd end on 30 June 1988 and a new AP is deemed to begin for both A Ltd and D Ltd on 1 July 1988. These deemed APs will then end, as normal, on 31 December 1988. Profits and trading losses are apportioned to the deemed APs thus created, on a time basis.

D Ltd
The amount of the trading loss of D Ltd available for group relief is thus:

	£
Trading loss for AP of 12 months	100,000
Trading loss for deemed AP of 6 months beginning 1 July 1988 being loss available for group relief: 1/2 × £100,00	50,000

A Ltd
The amount of the profit of A Ltd available for group relief is:
Total profits for AP of 12 months:

	£
Schedule D Case I	280,000
Schedule A	25,000
Chargeable gain	14,000
Total profits	319,000
Total profits for deemed AP of 6 months beginning 1 July 1988 being profits available for group relief: 1/2 × £319,000	159,500

Since the loss available to surrender (£50,000) is smaller than the profits available for relief (£159,000), the relief is restricted to the amount of the loss (£50,000). The corporation tax computations of the companies concerned are then:

A Ltd

	£
Schedule D Case I	280,000
Schedule A	25,000
Chargeable gain	14,000
Total profits	319,000
Less: Group relief	50,000
Profits chargeable to corporation tax	269,000

B Ltd

	£
Schedule D Case I and profits chargeable	50,000

D Ltd

	£
Schedule D Case I loss	100,000
Less: Utilised by way of group relief	50,000
Balance of loss available for carry forward (S.393(1))	50,000

In the above computation, it was assumed that the whole of the loss available for relief £50,000 was surrendered to A Ltd. However, part of the loss could also have been surrendered to B Ltd. In the circumstances set out in Example 6, the maximum claim which B Ltd could make on D Ltd is restricted to £25,000 – i.e., the profits of B Ltd for the deemed AP which began when D Ltd joined the group. Assuming B Ltd were to claim the maximum group relief possible (£25,000) the balance of the loss then available for surrender by D Ltd (also £25,000) could still be claimed by A Ltd. In short, a loss available for group relief may be claimed by one or a number of group companies subject to the limit of the smaller of the profit to be relieved in the case of each claimant company and the loss available. There can, of course, be no question of having losses allowed twice (S.411, TA 1988).

It will be noted that in Example 6 where apportionments have been required as a result of D Ltd joining the group on 1 July 1988 these have been calculated on a *time basis*. As a general rule, the Inland Revenue accepts that wherever a company enters a group apportionments of profits or losses should be carried out in this way. However, if time apportionment operates 'unreasonably or unjustly' some other 'just and reasonable' method can be used (S.409, TA 1988).

Although we have stressed the nature of the maximum group relief which may be obtained by a claimant company, the amount which is in fact claimed need not be the full amount which it is possible to claim (S.412(1)(a), TA 1988). This is in contrast to loss relief claims within a company itself (e.g., S.393(1), TA 1988 loss claims), where the maximum relief available has to be taken at the earliest moment.

5.2.5 Relation of group relief to other relief: the claimant company

We have talked so far of the right to set off group relief against the total profits of a claimant company. Examination of the corporation tax work form in Appendix 1 shows that group relief is the final deduction that is made in a corporation tax computation. That is to say, charges, trading losses brought forward under S.393(1), TA 1988 and trading losses of the current AP (S.393(2), TA 1988) are all deducted before group relief is given. There is, however, one major exception to the general rule that group relief is the final deduction to be made in the computation of profits chargeable to corporation tax. This exception concerns trading losses carried back from a subsequent AP under the provisions of S.393(2). These must be deducted *after* group relief has been given.

Example 7

Province Ltd is the wholly owned subsidiary of Empire Ltd. Both companies are trading companies which make up their accounts annually to 30 June. The following are the summarised results of the two companies for the 2 years ended 30 June 1988.

Years ended 30 June	1987 (£)	1988 (£)
Empire Ltd		
Schedule D Case I (loss)	(172,000)	(50,000)
Province Ltd		
Schedule D Case I profit/(loss)	(26,000)	67,000
Chargeable gains		1,000
Charges on income:		
Trade	2,000	2,000
Non-trade	500	500

In relation to the year to 30 June 1988, the parent company, Empire Ltd, is the surrendering company and Province Ltd, the subsidiary company, the claimant company. Since both companies made losses in the year ended 30 June 1987, there is no question of group relief in that year.

Group relief is available for the year ended 30 June 1988 as follows:

Empire Ltd
Trading loss AP ended
30 June 1988, available for relief   £50,000

Note:

It may be assumed that Empire Ltd is carrying forward for set-off against future trading income (under S.393(1), TA 1988) the trading loss of £172,000 realised in the year ended 30 June 1987. A trading loss being carried forward like this is not available for group relief – i.e., the loss available for relief in the AP ended 30 June 1988 is *not* £50,000 + £172,000 = £222,000.

Province Ltd
Profit available for relief:

	£	£
Schedule D Case I		67,000
Less: Loss brought forward (S.393(1))	26,000	
Trade charges brought forward (S.393(9) and S.393(1))	2,000	28,000
		39,000
Chargeable gain		1,000
		40,000
Less: Charges (trade and non-trade)		2,500
		37,500

Since the profit available is smaller than the loss available, the amount of group relief which may be claimed is limited to the profit, £37,500.

The computations for the two companies for the year ended 30 June 1988 will be as follows:

Empire Ltd

	£
Schedule D Case I (loss)	50,000
Less: Utilised Province Ltd	37,500
	12,500
Add: Brought forward (S.393(1), TA 1988)	172,000
Carried forward (S.393(1), TA 1988)	184,500

Province Ltd

	£	£
Schedule D Case I		67,000
Less: Brought forward (S.393(1), TA 1988)	26,000	
Trade charges brought forward (S.393(9) and S.393(1))	2,000	28,000
		39,000

Chargeable gain	1,000
Total profits	40,000
Less: Charges (trade and non-trade)	2,500
Profits chargeable	37,500
Less: Group relief	37,500
	Nil

5.2.6 Payment for group relief

In most cases where subsidiaries involved in a group relief claim are wholly owned by a parent holding company, there will be no question of payment by the claimant company for the benefit of the losses made available by the surrendering company. In other cases, however, particularly where a minority outside shareholder is involved, the claimant company may make a payment to the surrendering company in respect of the group relief received. Such a payment is not taken into account in the corporation tax computation of either company involved, and will not be treated as a distribution made by the claimant company or as a charge on the claimant's income (S.402(6), TA 1988).

5.3 GROUP INCOME AND INTEREST

A 51% subsidiary of a United Kingdom company may elect under S.247, TA 1988 to pay dividends to its parent company or to a fellow 51% subsidiary without accounting for ACT. The dividends passing between them are not treated as franked payments made by the subsidiary, or as FII of the recipient. Such dividends, paid under election, are called 'group income' of the recipient.

A 51% subsidiary is one in which more than 50% of the ordinary share capital is held by its parent. For the purposes of these provisions, there are no further special requirements concerning the interests of equity holders in distributions or assets.

An election may also be made under S.247 for intra-group charges to be paid without deduction of income tax. This election may be applied both to payments by a 51% subsidiary up to its parent and also to payments by a parent down to its 51%

subsidiaries, as well as to payments between fellow subsidiaries.

The consequences and disadvantages of not making a group election are illustrated in Example 8.

Example 8

Parent Ltd and Sub Ltd prepare accounts to 31 March each year. On 30 April 1988, Parent Ltd paid a dividend of £3,600. On 26 August 1988, Sub Ltd paid a dividend of £2,400 to Parent Ltd, of which it is a wholly owned subsidiary. If there is no S.247 election in force, the procedure for dealing with the ACT will be as follows:

(a) Parent Ltd will account to the Collector of Taxes for ACT on the dividend paid on 30 April 1988. Assuming it has no FII in this return period, Parent Ltd will pay ACT of £1,200 by 14 July 1988.

(b) Sub Ltd will account to the Collector of Taxes for ACT on the dividend paid on 26 August 1988. A payment of £800 will be sent to the Collector by 14 October 1988.

(c) Parent Ltd will send to the Collector a form CT61 in respect of the return period ended 30 September 1988, showing a dividend received on 26 August 1988. This FII will be set off against the franked payment made by Parent Ltd on 30 April 1988, and the tax credit of £800 will be repaid by the Collector of Taxes to Parent Ltd.

Had Parent Ltd and Sub Ltd made the group election, the cumbersome roundabout of payment and repayment of ACT would have been avoided. In practice, a group holding company will call up dividends from its wholly owned subsidiaries shortly before it pays its regular dividends. Having these paid under election maximises the group's cash flow, and minimises the number of administrative procedures.

Example 9

Older Ltd owns 55% of the shares in Younger Ltd. Both companies prepare accounts to 31 December each year. On 13 April 1988, Younger Ltd paid a dividend of £36,000 to Older Ltd. On 6 July 1988, Older Ltd paid a dividend of £53,250. A S.247 election is in force. The procedure for accounting for ACT can be stated simply:

(a) Younger Ltd pays a dividend to Older Ltd on 13 April 1988. A S.247 election is in force, and therefore no ACT is payable.

(b) Older Ltd pays a dividend to the shareholders on 6 July 1988. The amount of the franked payment is £53,250 + (25/75 × £53,250) = £71,000. Since a S.247 election is in force, Older Ltd does not have any FII available to set off against the franked payment because group income is not FII. Older Ltd will thus pay to the Collector the ACT on the dividend, which amounts to £17,750. This sum is payable by 14 October 1988.

In Example 9, where an election is in force, Older Ltd is liable for ACT of £17,750 on paying a dividend on 6 July 1988. Had no election been made:

		£
Younger Ltd would have paid ACT on its dividend of 13 April to Older Ltd – 25/75 × £36,000		12,000

Older Ltd would have paid ACT on its dividend of £53,250 of 6 July to its shareholders as follows:

	£	
Franked payment	71,000	
FII	48,000	
	23,000	
ACT @ 25%		5,750
Total ACT payable		17,750

As you will observe, whether or not an election is in force the group pays the same amount of ACT.

However, the *dates of payment* differ in an important way.

With no election, tax of £12,000 is payable on 14 July 1988 and £5,750 on 14 October 1988. With an election, the whole tax of £17,750 is payable on 14 October 1988. The cash flow benefit of an election in this instance and on these facts is the postponement of payment of £12,000 tax for 3 months (from 14 July 1988 to 14 October 1988).

The procedure for making group income and group interest elections is outlined in Ss.247(1) and 248, TA 1988. The election is made *jointly* by the paying company and the receiving company. The election is not effective until 3 months after it is made (or, if earlier, the date on which the Inspector of Taxes notifies the companies concerned that the conditions for the making of an election are satisfied).

From time to time a subsidiary company which has received some FII (or UFII) will find it more advantageous to pay a dividend (or a charge – e.g., debenture interest) outside of a group election. In these circumstances, the company informs the Collector of Taxes that it does not wish the election to apply.

Let us assume that in Example 8, Sub Ltd had a surplus of FII of £1,000 brought forward to the year ended 31 March 1989. The only way in which the group can obtain the benefit of the tax credit in

Sub Ltd's FII is to set it off against franked payments. The benefit of the tax credit, which is to reduce or eliminate a payment of ACT in the first instance, is a cash flow benefit. This cannot be realised unless a way can be found of transferring the benefit of the tax credit in Sub Ltd's FII to Parent Ltd. This is achieved by Sub Ltd making a franked payment – i.e., a payment outside the election with notification to the Collector. Parent Ltd then receives £1,000 of FII from Sub Ltd, and this reduces its liability to pay ACT in respect of its franked payments.

The computation would then proceed along the following lines:

> *Sub Ltd*
> (a) Part of dividend to be dealt with under normal rules:

	£
Dividend paid	750
Add: ACT	250
Franked payment	1,000
Less: FII available	1,000
Excess	Nil
ACT payable	Nil

> (b) Part of dividend to be dealt with under S.247 procedure:
>   Dividend paid £(2,400 − 750) = £1,650

> *Parent Ltd*
> (a) FII received £1,000 (i.e., the amount of Sub Ltd's franked payment). Set FII against franked payment made (30 April 1988) and obtain repayment of tax credit of £250.
> (b) Group income received £1,650.

Group income, which but for the S.247 election would be franked investment income, is *not* included in the profits of the recipient, i.e. the parent company, chargeable to corporation tax. By way of contrast group interest, which apart from the election would be unfranked investment income *is* included (as is UFII of course) in the corporation tax profits of the recipient company.

Example 10
Welshire Ltd has 3 subsidiaries: X Ltd, Y Ltd and Z Ltd. The following information is provided for the year ended 31 March 1989;

	£
Schedule D Case I profit	80,000
Schedule A	2,600

UFII	3,000
Group interest (representing loan interest payable by X Ltd under a S.247 election)	9,000
Group income (representing a dividend paid by Z Ltd under a S.247 election)	17,000

Corporation tax computation:

Schedule D Case I	80,000
Schedule A	2,600
UFII	3,000
Group interest	9,000
Corporation tax profits	94,600

Corporation tax payable:

£94,600 × 25%	23,650
Less: Income tax suffered on UFII	750
	22,900

Notes:
(1) Group income is not taken into account when ascertaining whether or not the small companies rate of tax is applicable (see Chapter 1).
(2) No income tax was deducted from the group interest so it is only income tax suffered in respect of the unfranked investment income that requires to be deducted from the corporation tax payable.

5.4 SURRENDER OF ACT

Advance corporation tax is set off against a corporation tax liability to arrive at corporation tax payable on the due date (mainstream corporation tax). ACT which is paid with respect to an AP is limited in amount, for the financial year 1988, to 25% of the company's profits for the accounting period.

Because of the restriction on the amount of ACT which can be deducted, more ACT may have been paid than it is possible to set off against a parent company's corporation tax liability and in such circumstances it is possible within a 51% group for a parent to surrender the surplus ACT for the accounting period in which the surplus arises to a 51% subsidiary (S.240 TA 1988).

The need for, and advantages of, such a provision are most obviously evident in the case of wholly owned subsidiaries. As we have already seen it is likely that subsidiaries will have paid dividends under a group election up to the group holding company without payment of ACT. It follows that while a subsidiary may well have a corporation tax liability it has no ACT to set against this liability (because of the group election), while a parent company may have a surplus of ACT which it cannot deduct from its corporation liability because of the 25% of profit restriction referred to above. From the group point of view this is an unsatisfactory state of affairs which the provision for surrender of ACT seeks to remedy.

S.240 TA 1988 allows a company which has paid advance corporation tax in respect of dividends paid by it, to surrender the ACT in whole or in part to its 51% subsidiary. Although a surrender will most often arise when there is a surplus of advance corporation tax in the parent company as described above, in theory there is no need for a surplus of ACT to exist; the parent could, if desired, surrender ACT rather than setting it off against its own corporation tax liability.

As we have seen a 51% subsidiary is one in which more than 50% of the ordinary share capital is held by its parent. In addition, the parent company must be beneficially entitled to more than 50% of profits available to equity holders and more than 50% of assets of the subsidiary available for distribution to equity holders were the subsidiary to be wound up (S.240(11) TA 1988). These and other anti-avoidance provisions in subsection 11 of S.240 will not usually be of relevance to normal commercial groups of companies.

Advance corporation tax which is surrendered by a parent to its 51% subsidiary is treated by the subsidiary as having been paid by it in respect of a distribution made by that subsidiary on the date when the actual dividend was paid by the parent company (S.240(2) and (3) TA 1988).

Surrendered ACT is available for set off against the corporation tax charged on the subsidiary. If the subsidiary is unable to utilise the full amount of the surrendered ACT in the current accounting period the surplus surrendered advance corporation tax may be carried forward by the subsidiary and set off against its corporation tax liability on profits in future accounting periods.

Example 11

Minnow Ltd is the 51% subsidiary of **Whale Ltd**. Both companies prepared accounts to 31 March each year. The following are the results for the year ended 31 March 1989.

Whale Ltd	£
Schedule D Case I	50,000
Chargeable gain	30,000
Ordinary dividend paid in March 1989	90,000
Related ACT	30,000

Minnow	
Schedule D Case I	15,000

Whale Ltd	
Corporation tax computation	
Schedule D Case I	50,000
Chargeable gain	30,000
Profits chargeable to corporation tax	80,000
Corporation tax at 25%	20,000
Less: ACT (maximum) 25% × £80,000	20,000
Mainstream corporation tax	Nil
Surplus ACT	
ACT paid	30,000
Maximum ACT deductible, 25% × £80,000	20,000
Surplus ACT	10,000

The surplus ACT of £10,000 (being part of ACT paid by Whale Ltd) may be surrendered to Minnow Ltd.

Minnow Ltd	£
Corporation tax computation	
Profits chargeable	15,000
Corporation tax at 25%	3,750
Less: ACT surrendered by Whale Ltd (maximum) 25% × £15,000	3,750
Mainstream corporation tax	Nil
Surplus ACT	
Advance corporation tax surrendered by Whale Ltd	10,000
Less: Utilised in year ended 31 March 1989	3,750
Surplus ACT available to Minnow Ltd. to carry forward	6,250

We have seen above that surrendered advance corporation tax may be carried forward by the subsidiary and utilised in subsequent years in the same way as if the subsidiary had paid the dividend and the resulting ACT itself. A company which has surplus ACT on its own account may also claim to have that surplus carried back for up to six years. A subsidiary which has a surplus of *surrendered* advance corporation tax may *not*, however, make a claim to have that surplus carried back.

Thus a subsidiary may carry back its own surplus ACT but may not carry back surrendered ACT. In these circumstances, if we are dealing with a subsidiary which has both surrendered advance corporation tax and advance corporation tax paid on its own account, we need to know which of the two amounts will be utilised in priority to set off against the corporation tax liability for the current accounting period. Section 240(4) TA 1988 provides that a surrendered amount of advance corporation tax will be set off against the subsidiary's liability to corporation tax for the current accounting period *before* ACT paid on a dividend actually paid by the subsidiary itself.

Example 12
Sub-Editor Ltd is the only 51% subsidiary of Editor Ltd. Both companies make up accounts annually to 31 March. The following are the results for Sub-Editor Ltd for the years ended 31 March 1988 and 1989.

Years ended 31 March	1988	1989
	£	£
Schedule D Case I profit	20,000	40,000
Dividend paid	—	15,000
ACT surrendered by Editor Ltd.		10,000
A single corporation tax rate of 25% will be assumed		

Sub-Editor Ltd
Corporation tax computation
Year ended 31 March 1989

Schedule D Case I profit	40,000
Corporation tax payable, £40,000 × 25%	10,000

Advance Corporation tax
ACT on dividend paid

£15,000 × 1/3	5,000	
Add: ACT surrendered by Editor Ltd	10,000	
Total ACT available	15,000	
Deduct: ACT set off, restricted to £40,000 × 25%	10,000	10,000
Surplus ACT	5,000	
Mainstream corporation tax		Nil

The advance corporation tax that has been set off in the year ending 31 March 1989 is £10,000. This is treated as being wholly the ACT surrendered by Editor Ltd, leaving £5,000 paid by Sub-Editor Ltd available to carry back to 1988.

Corporation tax computation	
Year ended 31 March 1988	£
Schedule D Case I profit	20,000
CT £20,000 × 25%	5,000
Less: ACT brought back from 1989	5,000
Mainstream corporation tax	Nil

5.5 TRANSFER OF CHARGEABLE ASSETS WITHIN GROUPS

Transfers of chargeable assets may be made within 75% groups without giving rise to any corporation tax charge on capital gains. A 75% group is defined with reference to ordinary share capital only and the 'equity holder' legislation does *not* apply.

A group for this purpose is defined in S.272(1) TA 1970 and means a company called a 'principal company' and all its 75% subsidiaries. If the subsidiaries themselves have 75% subsidiaries the definition of group member embraces these further subsidiaries and so on. A principal company means a company of which another is a 75% subsidiary.

Example 13
The following is the diagramatic representation of a group of companies. The percentages indicated are the percentage holdings of ordinary share capital owned by the parent in the relevant subsidiary:

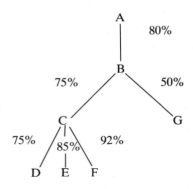

Since companies A, B and C each have 75% subsidiaries, A, B and C
are principal companies, as defined. Each principal company and its
75% subsidiaries forms a group for the purposes of the rules
regarding the transfer of chargeable assets within 75% groups. Thus
A and B are a group; B and C are a group; C and D E and F are a
group; moreover since B, a 75% subsidiary of A, has itself a 75%
subsidiary, C, which in turn has three 75% subsidiaries, D, E and F,
the group of A and B is extended to include C, D, E and F. This
means that company F for example, can transfer a chargeable asset to
company A without any tax charge on a capital gain.

The intention of the legislation regarding capital gains and
groups of companies is that all the companies within the same 75%
group should be treated as if they were a single entity. Transfers of
chargeable assets between companies within the group do not give
rise to chargeable gains or allowable losses.

Example 14

Alpha Ltd and Beta Ltd prepare accounts to 31 March each year.
On 10 January 1972 Alpha Ltd acquire a small office block at a cost of
£110,000.
On 4 June 1986 Alpha Ltd transfers the office block to Beta Ltd, one
of its wholly owned subsidiaries. The market value of the office block
at that time is £175,000.
On 6 September 1988 Beta Ltd sells the office block to Mr Roger – an
individual unconnected with the group. The sale proceeds are
£250,000.
Beta Ltd has sold a chargeable asset and is treated as having acquired
that asset in January 1972, the date of acquisition by Alpha Ltd, at a
cost of £110,000. Thus the full amount of the gain arising during the
whole of the period of ownership by the group is liable to tax in Beta
Ltd.

If a group company to which an asset has been transferred under the above provisions subsequently leaves the group within six years of the date of the transfer, the transferee company is deemed to have disposed of the asset on the date on which it acquired it. Thus a chargeable gain may arise covering the period from the original date of acquisition by the group to the date of transfer although the chargeable asset has not at the time the subsidiary leaves the group, been sold (S.278 TA 1970).

Example 15

Assume the same facts as in Example 14 except that we are now told that Alpha Ltd sold its 100% holding in Beta Ltd in February 1987, i.e. Beta left the Alpha group in February 1987.

The corporation tax computation of Beta Ltd for the year ended 31 March 1987 will include a chargeable gain calculated under S.278 TA 1970 as follows (ignoring indexation allowance):

	£
Market value at date of transfer from Alpha Ltd to Beta Ltd	175,000
Less: Cost 10 January 1972	110,000
Chargeable gain	65,000
Chargeable gain	65,000
Less: Abatement S.93 FA 1972, £65,000 × 1/7	9,286
Chargeable gain included in computation	55,714

It should be noted that a computation under S.278 TA 1970 is not required if a company ceases to be a member of a group as a result of being wound-up or dissolved.

5.6 CONSORTIA

We have seen above that the reliefs available to groups of companies apply where there is a parent company or holding company with a number of subsidiaries.

Two of the reliefs that we have considered are extended to consortia of companies, namely:

(a) Group relief for trading losses and charges etc. (S.402 TA 1988) and

(b) Payments of dividends and charges gross under a S.247 TA 1970 election.

A feature of modern commercial transactions has been the coming together of a number of previously unconnected companies to carry out an activity. The companies form a *consortium* and the activity is carried out by a trading company owned by the consortium or by a trading company owned by a holding company which in turn is owned by the consortium members.

A company is owned by a consortium if 75% or more of its ordinary share capital is beneficially owned by UK resident companies, none of which owns less than 5%.

Example 16

T. Ltd is a trading company whose ordinary share capital is owned equally by ten companies, eight of which are resident in the UK and two of which are resident in the USA. Since 80% of the ordinary share capital of T. Ltd is owned by UK resident companies, T. Ltd is a consortium company and the ten companies mentioned above are consortium members. It should be noted, however, that although the two US resident companies are members of a consortium they may not obtain the consortium reliefs since these are reserved to UK resident companies.

5.6.1 Surrender of trading losses

Consortium relief for trading losses is available between a consortium member, and vice versa (S.402 TA 1988). A loss incurred by a consortium trading company may be surrendered to consortium members in proportion to their percentage shareholdings in the trading company. When calculating the amount of loss available to surrender it must be assumed that the consortium company has claimed the maximum amount of relief under S.393(2) TA 1988. Likewise a loss incurred by a member of a consortium may be surrendered down to a consortium company and set off against a proportion of the latter company's profits. In this case the proportion of the profits which are available for relief is based on the percentage shareholding of the consortium member in the consortium company.

If a consortium member is also a member of a group of companies and is entitled to claim consortium relief in respect of a loss incurred by a consortium company, the relief may be passed on to any other company within the same group. Likewise if a company within the same group as the consortium member has incurred a loss, that loss may be surrendered through the consortium member to be set off against a proportion of the profits of the consortium company.

Example 17
Z. Ltd is a consortium company which makes up accounts annually to 31 March. In the year ended 31 March 1987 Z. Ltd makes a loss for consortium relief purposes of £100,000. The percentage ordinary shareholdings of Z. Ltd owned by the companies indicated are as follows:

	%
F Ltd	15
G Ltd	25
H Ltd	20
I Ltd	25
M Ltd	15

Subject to the matter of corresponding accounting periods each company will be entitled to claim its percentage share of the loss of Z Ltd by way of group (consortium) relief. Thus F Ltd may claim up to 15% of £100,000, i.e. £15,000 and so on for the other companies. Assume that F Ltd is part of a separate group of companies for example because it has two wholly owned subsidiaries A Ltd and B Ltd. If F Ltd has insufficient profits available for relief the right of F Ltd to claim relief for the loss of £15,000 may be passed on to any of the two other companies within the group – A Ltd or B Ltd.

It should be noted that if, in another later year, H Ltd incurred a loss, a proportion of that loss could be surrendered to Z Ltd. In this case since H Ltd owns 20% of the shares in Z Ltd the maximum amount of loss which may be surrendered is restricted to 20% of the profits of Z Ltd. (The provisions of S.406 TA 1988 would also apply to permit any company within the same group as H Ltd – assuming H Ltd to be within a group – to surrender a loss through H Ltd to be set off against 20% of the profits of Z Ltd). There is one further provision which relates to a company which is both a member of a group and a consortium company, for example a consortium trading company with one or more 75% subsidiaries. A loss arising to such a company is to be claimed first under S.393(2) TA 1988, second against the profits of group companies, and third against the relevant proportions of profits of consortium members.

5.6.2 Payment of dividends and charges under S.247 election

The group income and group interest provisions of S.247 TA 1988 are extended to consortia of companies. This means that:

(a) A trading or holding company owned by a consortium may pay dividends to any consortium member without accounting for advance corporation tax, and
(b) A trading or holding company owned by a consortium may pay charges to any consortium member without deducting income tax.

All the points discussed in relation to S.247 in a 51% group context apply equally to a consortium of companies.

Question 5

T Ltd owns 100% of the ordinary share capital of H Ltd, 80% of that of M Ltd and 60% of that of D Ltd. The companies have the following results for the 12 month chargeable accounting period ended 31 December 1989:

	T Ltd (£)	H Ltd (£)	M Ltd (£)	D Ltd (£)
Case I income	100,000	(15,000)	20,000	10,000
Capital gains	30,000	(5,000)	3,000	3,000
Case I losses brought forward	125,000	—	—	—
Dividends paid	60,000	12,000	—	—
Group income	12,000	—	—	—
FII – inclusive of tax credit	5,000	—	—	—
Charges on income paid (gross)	40,000	10,000	—	—

The following additional points of information have been obtained:

1. All the shareholdings in the four companies, other than those referred to above as being owned by T Ltd, are held by individuals.
2. The group income of £12,000 of T Ltd is the receipt of the dividend paid by H Ltd.
3. ACT on the dividend paid by T Ltd has been duly accounted for after taking account of the FII received by that company.
4. Income tax on the two amounts of charges on income paid has been duly accounted for.

Assume the following:

Corporation tax	35%
ACT	1/3
Income tax	25%

Required:

1. Explain, in the context of corporation tax, the meaning of the term 'group income' and 'group relief'.
2. Calculate the outstanding corporation tax liabilities, if any, of each of the four companies on the assumption that the desired aim is for the group as a whole to pay the minimum of taxation.
3. State what unutilised losses, if any, are available for carry forward at 31 December 1989.

CHAPTER 6

CLOSE COMPANIES

6.1   THE NATURE OF CLOSE COMPANIES

Many family companies are what the Taxes Act calls close
companies. A close company, broadly, is one which is under the
control of 5 or fewer of its shareholders or is under the control of
those shareholders who are its directors, even if there are more
than 5 of them (S.414(1), TA 1988).

This is not the place to trace the history and development of the
joint stock company, nor of the concept of the 'one man'
company. It is sufficient to observe that legally a single individual
(with another perhaps nominee shareholder) can *incorporate* his
business, and thereby create a legal person distinct from himself,
with separate powers, rights and liabilities. This fact has important
implications for taxation. What it means is that an individual who
conducts a business as an individual is subject to the income tax
code involving progressive rates of income tax, while the same
individual who forms a company may conduct the same business
through the agency of the company subject to the corporation tax
code with a single proportional rate of corporation tax. At higher
rates of income tax it will, other things being equal, be advantageous for a business to be carried on by a company rather than by a
sole trader or partnership. The exact point at which the advantage
lies with trading as a company depends on the facts of each case.

Because of the opportunities for tax avoidance using companies
in this way, and so as to maintain horizontal equity (equality of the
tax burden between taxpayers in similar positions) there is a
substantial body of legislation concerning the special class of
company controlled by a few persons which we have identified
above. The purpose of this anti-avoidance legislation was broadly
to ensure that cash received by shareholders in an otherwise tax
advantageous way – e.g., by way of a loan – should suffer a tax
charge, and that a company should adopt an adequate dividend

policy so that income should reach shareholders and be subject to higher rate income tax in their hands. In pursuit of the latter object the legislators imposed distribution standards which if they were not attained could result in income being apportioned (for tax purposes only) among the company's shareholders. Prior to 1980 these dividend standards were a consideration for a very large number of trading companies. Since 1980, for reasons inherent in the calculation of the distribution standard, family trading companies, while remaining close companies by definition, have been removed from what most would regard as the major effect of the legislation (although remaining subject to other minor rules); however, for trading companies accumulating and investing cash surpluses, and investment companies (including property investment companies), the whole body of legislation retains something of its earlier significance.

It is necessary to establish at the outset what is and what is not a 'close company'. Our consideration of the definition will require us to look at further special meanings given to words in the definitions and other special features of the legislation. In later sections of this chapter we shall consider the consequences for a company and its shareholders of being found to be 'close'.

6.1.1 Close company: definition

The words of S.414(1), TA 1988 define a close company as follows:

> *a close company is one which is under the control of five or fewer participators or of participators who are directors.*

Another definition of a close company is discussed in 6.8.

6.1.2 Participator

A 'participator' can for many practical purposes be thought of as a shareholder, but the definition in S.417(1) is much wider and embraces not only those who at present possess shares but also those who are or will be entitled to acquire shares, e.g., by means of a present option or a right to a future option to buy shares. A participator is

> *a person having a share or interest in the capital or income of the company.*

This definition includes an important class of persons described as 'loan creditors'. A loan creditor is defined in S.417(7), and includes someone having loan capital of the company – e.g., a debenture holder – as well as someone who simply advances money to a company on a loan account. It may be wondered how a lender of money to a company can be said to 'control' the company (see definition of close company above). However, 'control' has a technical meaning in the context of the legislation and means, in addition to more obvious meanings like voting control, an entitlement to receive more than half the assets of the company on a winding up (see 6.1.3). In this way, loan creditors, who are participators by definition, can control a company.

A bank lending money to a company in the ordinary course of business is not a loan creditor for the purposes of the definition or a participator.

6.1.3   Control

A person or persons have control of a company if they exercise control or are able to exercise control, or are entitled to acquire control, direct or indirect over the company's affairs (S.416(2), TA 1988). Control may be 'exercised' for this purpose in the following ways:

(1) The possession of, or the right to acquire:
    (a) the greater part of the share capital, or
    (b) the greater part of the issued share capital, or
    (c) the greater part of the voting power in the company, or
(2) The possession of, or the right to acquire, such part of the issued share capital as would result in an entitlement to more than half the income of the company if the whole of the company's income were distributed among the participators of the company. For this purpose, a loan creditor is not to be regarded as a participator; or
(3) The right to receive more than half the company's assets on a winding up or in any other circumstances.

An entitlement to acquire control means not only a present entitlement but also a *future entitlement* (S.416(4), TA 1988).

6.1.4 Associate

For the purpose of determining what person or persons have control, as defined, of a company, you must ascribe to a participator the powers and rights of his nominees and of any associate of that participator. An associate is defined in S.417(3), TA 1988, and means:

(a) a 'relative', that is husband or wife, parent or remoter direct ascendant – e.g., grandfather, grandmother, child or remoter direct descendant, or brother or sister,

(b) a partner,

(c) the trustees of any settlement set up by the participator or by one of the participator's relatives (as defined in (a) above),

(d) the trustees of a trust holding shares of the company or the personal representatives of a deceased person holding shares if the participator has an interest in these shares (e.g., as a beneficiary of the trust).

A participator may also have attributed to him the powers of a company which he, or he and his associates, control.

Attributions of power have to be made in such a way as will result in the company being under the control of 5 or fewer participators if this is possible.

Example 1

A company has the following share capital which is authorised, issued and fully paid:

10,000 ordinary shares of £1 each	£10,000

The shareholders and their respective shareholdings are as follows:

A	1,000
B (Wife of A)	500
C	1,500
D (Brother of A)	1,000
E	500
Z Ltd	900

and 20 other shareholders each holding 230 shares.
The share capital of Z Ltd is owned by A, B, C, D and E equally.

Who has control?

All the shareholders are participators as defined. Control for the purpose of the legislation is exercised by those who possess the

Corporation tax

greater part of the share capital of the company. Without regard to the question of associates and attribution of powers, control is exercised by the following persons (taking the holdings in descending order of magnitude):

C	1,500
A	1,000
D	1,000
Z Ltd	900
B	500
E	500
	5,400

Since the share capital (authorised and issued) is 10,000 shares, the 6 persons listed above, on this basis, have control.

Attributing to shareholder A the shareholdings of associates has the following results:

Attribution to A	
From wife B	500
From brother D	1,000
From Z Ltd, controlled by A and associates (60% 'owned' by A, B and D)	900
	2,400

Control is then exercised by the following:	
A – own holding	1,000
– attribution	2,400
	3,400
C	1,500
E	500
	5,400

The company for the purposes of close company legislation is thus under the control of 3 participators and is accordingly close.[1]

Even if a company falls within the primary definition of a close company (control by 5 or fewer participators, etc.) it may not be a close company for the purposes of the legislation. The exceptions are as follows:

(a) Companies not resident in the United Kingdom.

[1] For a reason which is discussed later (see 6.8), even if no shareholder were associated with another, the company would still be close.

(b) A registered industrial and provident society or a building society.

(c) A company controlled by or on behalf of the Crown, and not otherwise a close company (S.414(1), TA 1988).

(d) A company where not less than 35% of the shares are held by the public and the shares have been quoted in the previous 12 months, and there have been dealings in the shares on a recognised stock exchange in the previous 12 months (S.415(1), TA 1988). Companies of this sort are subject to further conditions which are discussed below.

(e) A company which is controlled by 1 or more non-close companies and the company cannot be considered as being controlled by 5 or fewer participators except by taking as one of the participators a non-close company (S.414(5), TA 1988).

Example 2

(a) An unquoted company has the following share capital:

Authorised	£50,000
Issued and full paid:	
42,000 ordinary shares of £1 each	£42,000

The shareholders are as follows:

A Ltd – a non-close company	22,000
M	14,000
N	4,000
O, sister of M	2,000
	42,000

A non-close company owns more than half of the issued share capital of the company, and accordingly a non-close company controls the company. There is no way in which the company may be considered close except by taking A Ltd, a non-close company, as one of the participators. Accordingly the company is not close.

(b) Suppose in the case of the company above that M has an option to subscribe for the 8,000 unissued shares of £1 each at £1.25 per share. As we have seen when we were considering who has control of a company, we must consider not only those who ⋆ possess shares but also those who are *entitled to acquire them*; moreover, the possession of more than half of a company's share capital as well as the possession of more than half of a company's issued share capital will give control. As regards the *issued* share capital of the company, the position is as in (a) above. The company is controlled by a non-close company and is itself non-close.

As regards the share capital of the company, which we may regard as the authorised share capital, a part of which is issued and a part of which M is entitled to have issued to him, the position is as follows:

M own holding (issued)	14,000
M own holding (option)	8,000
Ascribed holding (sister)	2,000
	24,000
N	4,000
	28,000

M and N accordingly control the company and the company is close. Note that with regard to the non-close company A, its holding of 22,000 shares does not give it control when we are considering the authorised capital of the company.

We see here that more than one person or group of persons can be said to control a company depending on what test you apply. Although A Ltd controls the company from the point of view of issued share capital, M and N also control it if you apply the authorised share capital test. Since the company on one of these tests can be found to be close, without taking account of A Ltd's shareholding, the company that we are considering is close.

6.1.5   Companies with a public interest

We have referred above to the fact that where at least 35% of the shares of a company are quoted and held by the public the company will not be close. The conditions of S.415, TA 1988 where the legislation is contained, are quite stringent. They are as follows:

(a) Shares carrying not less than 35% of the voting power of the company must be held by 'the public' (see below).

(b) The shares must not be shares entitled to a fixed rate of dividend – e.g., preference shares.

(c) The shares must have been dealt in on a recognised stock exchange within the preceding 12 months and the shares in that time must have been included in the official list of a recognised stock exchange.

(d) The voting power possessed by the company's 'principal members' must not exceed 85% (see below).

Shares are held by 'the public' if they are held by:

(a) a non-close company or a non-resident company which would not be close if it were resident, or
(b) trustees for approved superannuation and retirement schemes, or
(c) someone other than a 'principal member'.

A person is a 'principal member' if he possesses more than 5% of the voting power of the company and he is one of the 5 persons who possess the greatest percentage of the voting power of the company (see below).

The following shareholdings are not to be considered as held by 'the public' (even if they fall into one of the categories above):

(a) shares held by a director or associate of a director,
(b) shares held by a company which is controlled by such a director or associate,
(c) shares held by an associated company of the company; a company is another's associated company at a given time if, at that time or at any time within one year previously, 1 of the 2 has control of the other, or both are under the control of the same person or persons (S.416(1), TA 1988).
(d) Shares held by a fund the capital or income of which is applicable for the benefit of employees or directors of the company, or the employees or directors of a company controlled by a director (see (b) above) or those of an associated company.

A 'principal member' is a person who possesses more than 5% of the voting power of a company including for this purpose any attribution of powers from nominees, associates, and controlled companies. In addition, where there are more than 5 members holding more than 5% of the voting power, a 'principal member' is one of 5 persons possessing the greatest percentage of the voting power of the company. There can be more than 5 principal members if 2 or more such members hold equal percentages. Thus if there are 2 who hold equal percentages the number of principal members is increased to 6, if there are 3, the number of principal members is 7, and so on.

Example 3

A quoted company has the following share capital which is author-ised, issued and fully paid: 500,000 ordinary shares of £1 each.

Each ordinary share is entitled to 1 vote, and thus the voting power of shareholders is determined by the number of shares held. There have been dealings in the shares in the last year, and the company has been quoted in the last year.

The shareholders, the directors, and their percentage holdings of shares are as follows:

		(%)	
A		5	(Director)
B (Wife of A)		5	
C (Son of A)		5	(Director)
D Ltd (Controlled by A)		15	
E (Cousin of A)		20	
F		5	(Director)
G		5	
Other shareholders holding less than 5% of share capital:			
Directors		3	
Others		37	40
			100

Company is controlled by:	(%)
A own holding	5
wife's holding	5
son's holding	5
D Ltd's holding	15
	30
E (cousin, therefore not an associate of A)	20
F	5
	55

The greater part of the company's share capital is held by 3 persons and the company is prima facie close.

The 'principal members' are as follows	(%)
A (including attributions)	30
E	20

There are only 2 persons, namely A and E, holding more than 5% of the voting power of the company and therefore only 2 principal members.

The percentage of shares held by 'the public' is as follows (excluding the percentage held by principal members, directors, companies controlled by directors and associates of directors).

		(%)
A	director or principal member	—
B	associate of director	—
C	associate of director	—
D	Ltd controlled by A, a director	—
E	principal member	—
F	director	—
G		5
	Other shareholders, excluding directors	37
		42

Since more than 35% of the voting power of the company is held by the public, and the voting power of its principal members does not exceed 85% and the other conditions of S.415, TA 1988 are satisfied or assumed to be satisfied, the company is non-close.

6.2 THE EXTENDED MEANING OF DISTRIBUTIONS

In Chapter 3, we considered the general nature of distributions. Because of the special character of close companies many payments and benefits, not within the general definitions of a distribution, were at one time treated as distributions when made by a close company. The purpose was to prevent cash or other benefits being received by a shareholder in a way which gave tax advantages to the shareholder. Of these many instances happily only one now remains – benefits for participators.

Any 'benefit' which is provided by the company to a participator – e.g., a house to live in, domestic services, etc. – is a distribution (S.418(2), TA 1988). A very important exclusion from this special category of distribution is expenses and other benefits taxed in the hands of employees or directors under the Schedule E rules contained in Ss.153–168, TA 1988.

In practice, most benefits afforded shareholders of a close company are enjoyed by them as employees or directors and not as simply participators.

There is a further exclusion for pensions, gratuities, etc. paid to the wife or children or a former director or employee.

Example 4

Waverley Ltd, a close company, employs a painter for general maintenance of the company's factory. He is instructed to paint the exterior of the house of Mrs Jeanie Deans who is a shareholder. She is not an employee. The cost to the company of the painter's wages while painting the house and the cost of other materials used is a distribution to Mrs Deans. Since it is a qualifying distribution ACT is payable. The distribution plus the tax credit is included in Mrs Deans' income.

Where the shareholder receiving the benefit is a resident United Kingdom company, and both the shareholder and the close company are fellow subsidiaries of a third resident company or one is the subsidiary of the other, no distribution arises when an asset is transferred from one to the other (S.418(5), TA 1988).

There is anti-avoidance legislation dealing with mutual arrangements between 2 or more close companies for each to benefit shareholders of the other or others (S.418(7), TA 1988).

6.3 LOANS TO PARTICIPATORS

A loan by a company to a shareholder or an associate of a shareholder – e.g., wife of a shareholder – is one way by which a close company could make cash available without the tax consequences of making a distribution. However, S.419(1), TA 1988 provides for the payment of an amount of tax calculated by applying to the amount of the loan the rate of ACT for the financial year in which the loan is made. Although the amount payable is calculated as ACT would be calculated, it is not in fact ACT, and is not deductible from corporation tax liabilities or otherwise treated as ACT.

The provisions extend to debts incurred by the shareholder to the close company, but debts for goods supplied in the ordinary course of business are excluded unless the credit given is exceptional or exceeds 6 months. If the borrower is a full time employee of the company, and does not hold more than 5% of the ordinary share capital (that is, he does not have a 'material interest'), a loan which, together with previous loans, does not exceed £15,000 is exempt from payment of tax. If the loan was made before 31 March 1971, the exemption will apply if the loan was made for the purchase of the borrower's main residence and did not exceed £10,000 in amount (S.420(2), TA 1988).

Where a loan which has been charged to tax is repaid in whole or in part, the relative tax will be repaid. A claim has to be made to the Inland Revenue within 6 years from the end of the year of assessment in which the repayment of the loan occurs.

All the above applies to an individual who is a participator; the charge to tax also arises on the making of loans by a close company in certain other exceptional circumstances, in particular to a shareholder which is a non-resident company.

The making of a loan as such has no consequences for an individual's income tax liability. That is to say, the individual is not treated as having received a distribution or indeed any other type of income.

Tax consequences for an individual shareholder do however arise when a loan to the shareholder is written off or forgiven. When this happens the shareholder is treated as having received an amount equal to the amount written off, grossed up. In other words, the written off amount is treated as if it were a net sum corresponding to a gross amount from which income tax had been deducted (S.421(1), TA 1988).

Example 5

Mannering Ltd is a close company. On 30 June 1984, it advanced £7,000 on loan to Walter Guy, an ordinary shareholder. Walter Guy holds 20% of the ordinary share capital of the company, and is not a director of the company. On 30 June 1987, Walter Guy repaid £2,000 and on 30 June 1988 the company wrote off the balance of the loan (£5,000), and have informed Mr Guy that he is released from his debt.

The relevant tax consequences of these transactions are as follows:

(1) The advance of £7,000 to Walter Guy will give rise to a tax payment by the company of $3/7 \times £7,000 = £3,000$.

(2) The repayment of £2,000 by Walter Guy will result in a claim by the company for a repayment of tax of $3/7 \times £2,000 = £857$.

(3) The writing off of £5,000 by the company will result in

$$£5,000 \times \frac{100}{75}$$

£6,666 (see below) being included in Walter Guy's total income for 1988/89.

	£
Gross amount	6,666
Less: Basic rate income tax 1988/89, 25%	1,666
Net amount	5,000

6.4 RELEVANT INCOME

We have seen how the legislation ensures that benefits and loans
involving participators of close companies are adequately taxed.
This and the following sections describe and illustrate the legislation which tries to make sure that if certain close companies (non-
trading or trading companies with investment, etc. income) make
no distributions to shareholders, or make what is thought to be too
small distributions, income tax may be charged on shareholders as
if adequate distributions had in fact been made. There are rules
which the Revenue apply for deciding what amount of a company's income for an AP should be distributed, and this amount
(which is called the company's 'relevant income') cannot exceed a
certain maximum. The legislation in Sched.19, TA 1988 uses the
computation of chargeable profit for corporation tax as the basis
for the relevant income computation adding qualifying dividends
in FII (not included in the computation of chargeable profits) and
deducting any capital gains.

In the case of a trading company (or a member of a trading
group) the relevant income is defined as

> so much of its distributable income, (the product of the computation
> outlined above) other than trading income ... as can be distributed
> without prejudice to the requirements of the company's business
> (Para.1(1)(a), Sched.19, TA 1988).

A *trading company* is:

    (a) a company which exists wholly or mainly to carry on a
        trade, or
    (b) a company whose income does not consist wholly or
        mainly of investment income – i.e., income which
        would be unearned income in an individual's hands.

Because the above definition excludes trading income arising to
trading companies from relevant income, most trading companies
in practice are effectively removed from the worst effects of being
a close company.

Let us suppose, however, that a long established trading
company with a successful profitable business begins to accumulate profits and invest these profits in shares or interest bearing
securities or rented properties. If this investment income is large

enough, then a trading company may have to introduce the notion of the 'requirements of the business' to show that it is unable to distribute the investment income.

In the case of a non-trading company whose income includes estate or trading income relevant income is:

(a) so much of the estate or trading income as can be distributed without prejudice to the requirements of the company's business so far as concerned with the activities or assets giving rise to estate or trading income.

(b) as far as the rest of the company's income is concerned – e.g., interest and dividends – the whole of that income (Para.1(1)(b), Sched.19, TA 1988).

It often happens that an investment company may have both estate income (income from land chargeable under Schedules A, B and D) and some trading income. In respect of both types of income 'business requirements' can be called in aid. You will note that unlike the position with trading companies, trading income of an investment company cannot be ignored.

Finally if an investment company has no estate or trading income the relevant income is the distributable income.

In all the cases above, relevant income is subject to an *arithmetical maximum*, which is discussed below.

6.4.1 Distributable income

The 'distributable income' of a company is the amount of the distributable profits *less* chargeable gains net of corporation tax. The amount of distributable profits is the total of the following:

(a) The amount of any profits on which corporation tax falls finally to be borne, *less* the amount of that tax. The amount of any profits on which corporation tax falls finally to be borne is the familiar amount of chargeable profits in a corporation tax computation. The corporation tax chargeable on these profits is deducted.

(b) An amount equal to the qualifying distributions comprised in any FII. You will remember that FII is *inclusive* of relative tax credits. The amount to be included in the total making up distributable profits is 'net' FII.

(c) An amount equal to group income; group income is a distribution from a 51% subsidiary in respect of which an election has been made such that no ACT is paid by the subsidiary and no tax credit is received by the parent (see 5.3).

Distributable income and distributable profits may be set out diagrammatically as follows:

	£	£
Chargeable profits		X
Less: corporation tax		X
		X
'Net' FII		X
Group income		X
Distributable profits		X
Less: Chargeable gains	X	
Less: Corporation tax	X	
		X
Distributable income		X

6.4.2 Business requirements

In the above discussion you will have found more than one reference to 'business requirements'. 'Business requirements' are not defined. However, not only current requirements are relevant. Regard is had 'to such other' requirements as may be necessary or advisable for the maintenance and development of that business (Para.1(2), Sched.19, TA 1988); in addition 'requirements necessary or advisable for the acquisition of a trade or of a controlling interest in a trading company' also fall within the category of a 'business requirement' of a trading company (Para.1(3), Sched.19, TA 1988).

The latter requirement is hedged about with anti-avoidance legislation concerning acquisitions of associated companies (Para.9, Sched.19, TA 1988).

Business requirements are the normal short and long term financial and commercial needs of the company. These might include:

(a) the company's need for working capital,

(b) a need to repay share or loan capital by a trading company; statutory provision is specifically made for this need in Para.1(3–5), Sched.19, TA 1988,

(c) the need to finance expansion of the company,

(d) the need to be able to meet the known and contingent liabilities of the company,

(e) the need to provide for depreciation and obsolescence of plant and machinery.

Non-trading companies with no estate or trading income cannot reduce relevant income by arguing that the company has business requirements.

A non-trading company with estate or trading income can claim business requirements with respect to that income. However such a company – for example, a property investment company with a rental income (estate income) – must regard as income available for distribution, sums applied or to be applied out of income in repayment of any loan capital or debt (e.g., bank loan), or in the purchase of land or on the construction or extension of a building (Para.8(1)(c) and (d), Sched.19, TA 1988). It is thus not possible to regard these payments or purchases as business requirements. This is very significant for property companies. Non-trading companies with estate or trading income claiming business requirements must also consider the legislation concerning repayment of what are called 'first business loans' – e.g., loans towards payment for the business undertaking or property which the company was formed to acquire (Para.8(1), Sched.19, TA 1988).

6.5 EXCESS OF RELEVANT INCOME OVER DISTRIBUTIONS

Having arrived at the amount of a company's relevant income for an AP (the amount which may be distributed without prejudice to the business), the rules require us to compare this amount of income with the distributions for the AP which have been made within the AP or within a reasonable time afterwards (Para.3, Sched.19, TA 1988). If relevant income for the AP is more than the distributions for the AP there is what is called 'an excess of relevant income over distributions' or simply 'an excess of relevant income'. The term 'shortfall', which derives from earlier legislation, is still used.

The excess of relevant income for an AP is apportioned among the participators of the company in accordance with their respective interests. This apportionment is not a payment of cash but a computation of the amount which, in a straightforward case, a shareholder might have received as a dividend, had there been a distribution of an amount equal to the excess of relevant income. Each shareholder is then deemed to have received as income, as at the end of the AP in which the shortfall arises, the apportioned amount plus a proportion corresponding to ACT on that amount. Further details of apportionments (and the consequences as regards the close company itself of an excess of relevant income) are to be found in 6.7 below.

Relevant income on cessation or liquidation
When a close company ceases to carry on a trade, or is wound up, relevant income will take no account of business requirements. The interests of creditors (other than creditors who are participators or associates of participators) will however, be safeguarded (Para.10, Sched.19, TA 1988).

6.6 MAXIMUM RELEVANT INCOME

We have referred from time to time to the fact that a close company's relevant income is limited to an *arithmetical maximum*. The method of computation of this amount is described in Para.2, Sched.19, TA 1988. The computation produces the maximum amount which may be regarded as relevant income. The details of the computation refer from time to time to kinds of income and other matters some of which we have already mentioned. The principles underlying the computation are as follows:

(a) For *trading companies*, the maximum relevant income is 50% of the company's estate income and 100% of the company's distributable investment income (Para.2, Sched.19, TA 1988).

(b) For *non-trading companies*, the maximum relevant income is 50% of estate or trading income and 100% of the company's distributable investment income (Para.2, Sched.19, TA 1988).

It follows from the above that for the purposes of the computation, a company's income has to be analysed between estate, trading and investment income. Because of other features of the computation it is necessary to extend the analysis of income.

Example 6
Lammermuir Ltd is a close property company which has the following results for the AP of 12 months ended 31 March 1989.

	£
Schedule D Case I	20,000
Schedule A	500,000
FII	30,000
UFII	1,000
Chargeable gains	40,000
Debenture interest paid (gross)	10,000

The computations of the company's relevant income and maximum relevant income are as follows:

	£
Relevant income	
Schedule D Case 1	20,000
Schedule A	500,000
UFII	1,000
	521,000
Less: Charges	10,000
	511,000
Less: Corporation tax at 35%	178,850
	332,150
'Net' FII £300,000 − (25% × 30,000)	22,500
Distributable income	354,650

Distributable income is arrived at in a manner similar to that discussed in 6.4.1. Instead of deducting chargeable gains net of corporation tax from distributable profits, chargeable gains have been excluded from the computation above, which gives the same result. As to charges, these are deducted from different kinds of income in a certain order (see below and Para.6(2) and (3), Sched.19, TA 1988; the effect of the rules is that in the above computation no part of the charges of £10,000 is deductible from the chargeable gain since this is excluded.
Relevant income is distributable income £354,650 *less* whatever amounts require to be retained for business requirements; if these requirements were £40,000 with respect to say, estate income,

Corporation tax

relevant income would be £314,650. Note that this latter figure cannot exceed the maximum figure of relevant income as follows:

Maximum relevant income

	Total	Investment income Estate or trading	FII (net)	UFII	Chargeable gain
	(£)	(£)	(£)	(£)	(£)
Schedule D Case I		20,000			
Schedule D		500,000			
FII			22,500		
UFII				1,000	
Chargeable gain					40,000
	583,500	520,000	22,500	1,000	40,000
Charges	10,000	9,000		1,000	
	573,500	511,000	22,500		40,000
CT at 35%	192,850	178,850			14,000
Distributable profits	380,650	332,150	22,500		26,000
Less: Chargeable gain	26,000				26,000
Distributable income	354,650	332,150	22,500		
Less: Lesser of £1,000 and 10% of estate or trading income			1,000		
Distributable investment income			21,500		
Estate or trading income		332,150			

Maximum is:

	£
50% of estate or trading income, 50% × £332,150	166,075
100% of distributable investment income, 100% × £21,500	21,500
	187,575

The computation of maximum relevant income contained in Example 6 flows directly from the requirements of the legislation. As we have seen, in the case of a non-trading company relevant income cannot exceed 50% of the estate or trading income and 100% of the company's distributable investment income. For this purpose both kinds of income are after tax, and in the above case after an abatement in respect of investment income in distributable profits of 10% of estate or trading income or £1,000 whichever is smaller (Para.4(2), Sched.19, TA 1988).

In the case of a *trading* company there is also an abatement in respect of investment income in the same form as above but the figure of £1,000 in the non-trading case is increased to £3,000 (Para.4(2), Sched.19, TA 1988).

A trading company enjoys a further important abatement with respect to estate income. It will be remembered that for a trading company trading income as such is deducted from distributable income and is not part of relevant income (and it follows is not part of maximum relevant income). However in the computation of the abatement of estate income referred to above we have, for calculation purposes only, to take account of trading income.

Let us assume that a trading company has trading income of £45,000 and estate income of £15,000 after deduction of corporation tax, etc. We first have to compute a fraction called in the legislation 'the appropriate fraction', which is:

$$= \frac{\text{Estate income}}{\text{Estate income} + \text{Trading income}}$$

$$= \frac{£15,000}{£15,000 + £45,000}$$

$$= 1/4$$

The factor of 1/4 is then applied to a maximum and minimum amount specified in the legislation, the latter being £25,000 and the former £75,000, that is:

	£
1/4 × £75,000 (maximum amount)	18,750
1/4 × £25,000 (minimum amount)	6,250

If the estate income of the company is less than the appropriate fraction of the minimum amount the estate income is disregarded –

i.e., 'abated' – by the whole amount of it. If the estate income is less than the appropriate fraction of the maximum amount it is abated by half the difference between the fractional part of the maximum amount and the amount of the estate income. In the above example estate income is thus £15,000. This is more than 1/4 × £25,000 (£6,250) and less than 1/4 × £75,000 (£18,750). Accordingly, the abatement is 1/2 (18,750–15,000) = £1,875.

All of the above is an expression by way of a computed example of the legislation contained in Para.2(2), Sched.19, TA 1988.

It may be more simply expressed as follows:

(1) If the aggregate trading and estate income is less than £25,000, the whole of the estate income is excluded.
(2) If the aggregate trading income (T) and estate income (E) is between £25,000 and £75,000, the estate income is abated by:

$$1/2 \times ((\frac{E}{E + T} \times £75,000) - E)$$

The above maximum and minimum amounts (£75,000 and £25,000) may be reduced if a company has associated companies (Para.2(3), Sched.19, TA 1988).

In Example 6, a division is made of investment income between UFII and FII. This division is between investment income chargeable to corporation tax (UFII) and FII which is not chargeable to corporation tax. The necessity to distinguish between, these two kinds of investment income arises from the treatment of charges in the computation of maximum relevant income.

Charges are deductible from total profits in a corporation tax computation. If we now divide these total profits between different kinds of income we need to have rules which will guide us in deducting charges from the different sorts of income. Para.6(2) and (3), Sched.19, TA 1988 contains two sets of rules, one for trading companies and one for non-trading companies. As regard non-trading companies the order is as follows:

(a) *first* from the company's income charged to corporation tax other than estate or trading income – e.g., UFII,
(b) *second* from the company's estate or trading income,
(c) *third* from development gains,
(d) *fourth* from chargeable gains.

For trading companies, the order is slightly amended, (a) and (d) remain as before; deduction (b) is from estate income and deduction (c) from trading income.

6.6.1 Cessations and liquidations

Where a close company ceases to trade or is wound up, the computation of the amount of the company's relevant income and maximum relevant income proceeds without reference to the requirements of the company's business and there is no limitation to 50% of estate or trading income (Para.10(1), Sched.19, TA 1988). These rules apply to the AP in which the trade ceases or which ends with the cessation of the trade or the winding up of the company. In addition they apply to all APs of the company ending within 12 months of the cessation or winding up, and in the latter case with any subsequent AP of the company (Para.10(6), Sched.19, TA 1988).

6.6.2 Inspector's clearance

A close company may prompt a review of its position for any year by submitting its accounts and directors report and other information to the Inland Revenue and seeking a statement from the Inspector of Taxes as to whether or not he intends to make an apportionment (Para.16, Sched.19, TA 1988).

6.7 APPORTIONMENT OF EXCESS

Example 7
In Example 6 above, we computed that the maximum relevant income of Lammermuir Ltd for the year ended 31 March 1989 was £187,575.
The share capital authorised issued and fully paid of Lammermuir Ltd is as follows:

200,000 ordinary shares of £1 each
The shareholders and their respective shareholdings are:

A	40,000
B (wife of A)	40,000
C (son of A)	40,000
D	20,000
E	8,000
F	52,000
	200,000

The dividend paid by Lammermuir Ltd in the year ended 31 March 1989 was:

Final dividend in respect of year ended 31 March 1988 £80,000

Since no dividend in respect of the year ended 31 March 1989 was paid in that year (and on the assumption that no such dividend is paid within a reasonable time after 31 March 1989), the excess of the relevant income over distributions is:

	£
Maximum relevant income	187,575
Less: Distribution	Nil
Excess of relevant income over distributions	187,575

The above excess is apportioned among participators in accordance with the respective interests of participators as follows:

	£
A 1/5	37,515.00
B 1/5	37,515.00
C 1/5	37,515.00
D 1/10	18,757.50
E 2/50	7,503.00
F 13/50	48,769.50
	187,575.00

The apportioned amounts are treated as income received by the shareholders at the end of the AP concerned – i.e., 31 March 1989. Furthermore, the amounts assessable are the same as if the company had paid a dividend – i.e., a proportion has to be added for 'ACT' at the rate which is in force at the year end (S.428(1), TA 1988).

A shareholder will be assessed to income tax on an apportionment only if the amount which has been apportioned to him (inclusive of ACT) is at least £1,000 or 5% of the total amount (plus ACT) to be apportioned among participators, whichever is the less.

Amounts which are apportioned to shareholders are assessable and charged to higher rate tax. No assessment is made at basic rate (S.426(2)(b), TA 1988). If the individual shareholders do not pay the tax within certain time limits the company can be required to pay the tax. Since no actual cash income is received by shareholders companies usually pay the tax arising on apportionments (S.429, TA 1988).

The apportionment of an excess of relevant income among

participators of a company has no effect on the corporation tax liability of the company. However there are provisions in S.430 TA 1988 which try to ensure that a close company does not obtain any cash flow advantage from waiting for a shortfall assessment rather than paying a dividend.

6.7.1 Excess of £1,000 or less

No apportionment is made where the excess of relevant income over distributions of a trading company is £1,000 or less (S.424(1)(b), TA 1988).

6.7.2 Apportionment of interest

Payments of interest which are annual payments – e.g., debenture interest made by a non-trading company – may be apportioned to shareholders whether or not there is an excess of relevant income over distributions.

There will be no apportionment if the interest would be allowed to an individual (S.353, TA 1988) or more than 75% of the company's income is estate or trading income as is the case in Example 6 above (Lammermuir Ltd) (S.424(3), TA 1988). This provision does not apply to trading companies.

6.7.3 Dividend restriction

Where a company is subject to dividend restriction by law – e.g., company law – no apportionment will be made of any excess of relevant income over distributions, to the extent that the company could not make distributions except by breaking the law (Para.11, Sched.19, TA 1988).

6.8 ANOTHER DEFINITION OF CLOSE COMPANY

A close company is usually a company under the control of 5 or fewer participators or of its directors. A further definition is contained in S.414(2), TA 1988. This provides that if on the assumption that the company is close (and any other company which is a participator is also close) more than half of any excess of

relevant income could be apportioned among 5 or fewer partici
pators or among participators who are directors, the company wil
be close.

In terms of this definition the company in Example 1 above i
close, even if no one shareholder were associated with any other

Question 6

Mortality Ltd is an old established trading company with a
successful profit record. The company, which is a close company
has been managed by the majority shareholders, a bachelor and
his brother, for more than 40 years. The company has no plans fo
expansion and cash surpluses have accumulated and continue to
accumulate in the company. Apart from debentures held by ar
aged sister, the company has no indebtedness. The following is the
company's corporation tax computation for the year ended
31 March 1989:

	£
Schedule D Case I	200,000
Schedule A	44,000
UFII	30,000
Schedule D Case III	12,000
Total profits	286,000
Charges	10,000
Profits chargeable	276,000

In addition, the company received £100,000 of FII.

The brothers are in receipt of substantial salaries and othe
private income and wish to receive as dividends as little as possible
from Mortality Ltd. They have asked you to advise on the
minimum dividend which they might receive from Mortality Ltd to
avoid any question of an apportionment.

As a first step in your considerations, you are required to
prepare a maximum relevant income computation for Mortality
Ltd for the year ended 31 March 1989.

CHAPTER 7

FOREIGN ELEMENT

7.1 INTRODUCTION

The tax jurisdiction of the British state extends to the land mass of Scotland, England, Wales, Northern Ireland and the UK territorial waters within the so-called 3 mile limit. Some extension of jurisdiction has been made to the continental shelf. The rest of the world (including the Channel Islands and the Isle of Man) lies beyond its authority.

Limits to taxing power imply that in any case it will be possible to say what income or profits are taxable by the authority and what items are not taxable by it. Wholly domestic companies naturally pose no problems but issues will arise wherever there is a foreign element – for example, a trade conducted abroad by a domestic company, or a trade conducted here by an overseas company. The general principle is that the UK seeks to tax the worldwide profits of UK resident companies and in addition profits which arise from a UK source – e.g., the UK branch of an overseas company. The questions of residence and source are thus key issues in the consideration of the foreign element which are considered later in this chapter.

In the context of international trade and investment it will often happen that two or more states will charge the same profits to taxation. For example, the profits of an overseas branch operated by a UK resident company will invariably be assessed under Schedule D Case I in the same way as a trade in the UK. In addition to being charged to UK corporation tax, the profits of the overseas branch will usually be charged to tax in the overseas country. Without a means of relief, the profits would be doubly and excessively taxed. To provide relief the UK has entered into numerous *double tax conventions* with other states, which override the effect of domestic legislation and which are an important aspect of the foreign element.

Although the vast majority of overseas investments undertake
by UK companies have a straightforward commercial motive,
would be unrealistic to suppose that low rates of tax and othe
benefits may not be either the dominant or a secondary concern c
the companies involved. The ending of exchange control and th
growth of international movements of capital and other resource
have caused the Treasury and the Inland Revenue to becom
concerned about the loss of tax revenue which has occurred. Th
UK authorities are not alone in their concern about the ways i
which companies may walk out of a state's territorial jurisdictior
and aspects of modern UK legislation dealing with this problen
mirror the legislation enacted in Japan and elsewhere. Thi
concern is not new and anti-avoidance legislation, in part unuse
in practice, has been on the statute book for some time. In 1984
legislation was introduced concerning controlled foreign com
panies (described as CFCs) where the companies are controlled b
UK residents and are resident in low tax areas. This aspect of th
legislation and its effect is of significance to tax havens and ta
avoidance activities.

7.2 RESIDENCE

Corporation tax is charged on UK resident companies, and on th
chargeable profits of a non-resident company which carries on
trade in the UK through a branch or agency (S.6(1) and (2) an
S.11(1), TA 1988).

7.2.1 Position before 15 March 1988

Before the passing of FA 1988, UK domestic legislation containe
no general definition of a company's residence. Over the year
since the end of last century there had built up a substantial bod
of case law on the subject. The distillation of these decisions wa
the finding that a company was resident where its central manage
ment and control resided. In practice, the country in which th
board of directors met was considered prima facie evidence tha
central management and control was exercised in that country.
As the law stood prior to 15 March 1988, the country o
incorporation was no more than a factor in deciding where i

ompany was resident. A company incorporated in Scotland with
UK shareholders (a 'Scottish' company) would thus be resident in
France for UK tax purposes if its central control and management
was in France. By the same token, a French incorporated company
(a 'French' company) would be resident in Scotland for UK tax
purposes if its central control and management was in Scotland.

.2.2 Position from 15 March 1988

In contrast with the situation outlined above, from 15 March 1988
the very fact of incorporation in the UK makes a company resident
in the UK for tax purposes. Except where a UK company was in
business before 15 March 1988, the place of central control and
management is irrelevant (S.66 FA1988).

However, the question of control and management remains
relevant to foreign companies – i.e., companies not incorporated
in the UK. In such cases, if central management and control is in
the UK the company will be resident in the UK on the basis of the
earlier principles.

After 15 March 1988, the rule is thus that a company is resident
in the UK for tax purposes if it was incorporated in the UK (a UK
company) or if the central management and control of the
company is in the UK (a foreign company).

Because of the very significant change concerning the residence
of UK registered companies, FA 1988 provided that where a UK
company was not resident in the UK immediately before 15 March
1988 (because of the central management and control principle) it
would not become resident in the UK by reason of its UK
incorporation until 15 March 1993 – 5 years after 15 March 1988.
However if central management and control of such a company is
transferred to the UK before 15 March 1993, it becomes resident
from that earlier date (Sched. FA 1988).

The significance of residence for companies as taxpayers should
not be lost sight of. Consider a US incorporated company with a
branch factory in East Anglia; if central management and control
of the company is (say) in New York, UK corporation tax will be
paid only on the trading profits of the UK branch; if central
management and control of the US company is (say) in Norwich,
then not only will the UK branch profits be subject to UK
corporation tax but the whole worldwide profits of the US

company will be liable to UK corporation tax because th
company is UK resident.

Likewise, if a company incorporated in England (say, in 1989
conducts a trade wholly abroad, it will be subject to UK
corporation tax on the profits of the overseas trade, even wher
the management and control of the trade is overseas.

Where it is desired that UK corporation tax be avoided wit
respect to an overseas trade or activity, the appropriate actio
would be to form an overseas subsidiary company – i.e.,
company incorporated overseas – and transfer the trade to th
overseas company. On the assumption that central managemen
and control of the subsidiary company is overseas and that th
board of directors also meets overseas, then the overseas sub
sidiary will be resident outside the UK.

It will be clear from the above that it is possible for a compan
resident in the UK to become non-resident – e.g., an oversea
company moves its central management and control in the UK t
an overseas country – and for a UK resident company (say, a UK
incorporated company) to transfer its trade to a foreign non
resident subsidiary.

To protect the revenue from loss in these kinds of circum
stances, TA 1988 and FA 1988 contain a number of importan
provisions concerning an 'exit charge' at the time a compan
ceases to be UK resident on a deemed disposal of the company'
assets, provisions for the payment of outstanding tax and in certai
circumstances, the obtaining of consents from the Treasury a
described in 7.5, 'Migration and Treasury Consents' below.

7.3 EXIT CHARGE

Where a foreign company resident in the UK ceases to be resident
FA 1988 provides that all the assets of the company are to be
deemed to have been sold and acquired at their market value with
the effect that any chargeable gains (for capital gains tax) are
deemed to be realised and subject to corporation tax at the
moment when the change of residence occurs. A limited form o
so-called 'roll-over relief' (a capital gains tax relief) may be
available (Ss. 105–107 FA 1988).

7.4 PAYMENT OF TAX

A foreign company ceasing to be UK resident has to comply with certain requirements contained in FA 1988 concerning payment of tax (including corporation tax and income tax due under PAYE regulations and various sections of the Taxes Act).

The FA 1988 regulations require that the company gives notice to the Board of Inland Revenue of its intention to cease to be resident, and requires it to provide a statement of the tax payable and the arrangements which the company has made for payment of the tax.

Failure to comply with the regulations can give rise to a penalty on the company of up to the amount of tax payable. A parent company and a director of the migrating company or its parent may each be liable to a penalty of up to the amount of tax payable if they have taken any action which causes the migrating company not to meet its obligations under the regulations.

Finally, when tax payable by the migrating company is not paid in accordance with the provisions of FA 1988, payment of tax and interest can be demanded of fellow group members, and from a controlling director of the migrating company or its parent (Ss. 130–132 FA 1988).

7.5 MIGRATION AND TREASURY CONSENTS

Certain actions taken without the consent of the Treasury are unlawful. These are contained in para.(1)(c) and (d), S.765, TA 1988:

> (c) for a non-resident company which is controlled by a resident UK company – e.g., an overseas subsidiary of a UK parent – to create or issue shares or debentures;
>
> (d) for a UK resident company to transfer to any person any shares or debentures which it owns in a non-resident company which it controls – e.g., sale by a UK parent of its shares in an overseas subsidiary (S.765(1), TA 1988).

The penalties for an offence under these provisions are heavy and – uniquely in UK tax legislation – provide specifically for the possibility of imprisonment for up to 2 years (or fines up to

£10,000). As a matter of fact, however, no prosecutions have taken place since 1951.

The above actions will not be unlawful if the Treasury give consent, and the Treasury may give consents *generally* or *specifically*. The general consents have been published and are summarised below. Special consents will apply only to a particular transaction or a particular company, and the information which the Treasury requires to make a decision is published. In the case of the general consents referred to above, no application to the Treasury for consent is necessary.

In respect of the unlawful action referred to in para.(c), general consents (called Treasury General Consents 1988) have been given for the controlled non-resident company to create shares and

    (i) to issue shares to another member of the overseas group;

   (ii) to issue irredeemable shares to the UK resident company (or member of the UK resident group) for cash or in purchase of a business;

  (iii) to issue shares for full consideration paid to the non-resident company to a person not connected with the UK resident company;

  (iv) to issue irredeemable shares in proportion to the shares held by the shareholders in the non-resident company. If no shares are issued to a UK company, the shares can be redeemable, but in such a case they must be issued for full consideration paid in cash.

Consent is also given in relation to the action in para.(c) if the non-resident company was incorporated after 31 December 1951 for the purpose of starting and carrying on a new industrial activity, and the company is liable to tax in a Commonwealth country.

Subject to a number of constraints and always in the context of the action in para.(c), a non-resident company may create debentures and issue them:

   (1) to another member of the overseas group;

   (2) to the UK resident company or another member of the resident group; among the conditions attached to this permission are that the debentures are not issued at a

discount, that amounts payable in respect of the debentures
are not determined by reference to any price index, and that
no loan is made by a non-resident UK company to a UK
resident company where the loan is associated with the issue
of the debentures;

(3) to persons not connected with the resident company where
the issue is for full consideration paid to the non-resident
company.

Consent is given in relation to the action in para.(d) which consists
of

    (i) the transfer by the resident company of shares or
debentures of the non-resident company to
another member of the resident group;

    (ii) the transfer by the resident company or by a non-
resident company to a person not connected with
the resident company for full consideration paid to
the transferor company;

    (iii) the transfer by a company which is not resident in
the UK to a non-resident group member of shares
or debentures of the non-resident company.

7.6 INWARD INVESTMENT

In considering the foreign element it is common to consider the
position under two aspects – that of the foreign resident company
investing in the UK, so called 'inward investment', and that of the
UK resident company investing overseas, that is to say 'outward
investment'. Many of the reflections which apply to inward
investment will apply to outward investment, and vice versa. We
shall look at inward investment first.

Corporation tax applies to the chargeable profits of a non-
resident company which carries on a trade in the UK through a
branch or agency. A 'branch or agency' means any factorship,
agency, receivership, branch or management (S.834, TA 1988). So
if Zavok Inc., an overseas manufacturer of cars, were to set up a
factory in the UK to assemble cars, this would be a branch of
Zavok Inc. and the profits of the branch would be liable to
corporation tax; so also if Zavok Inc. instead of acquiring a

factory, etc. were to appoint a resident UK individual as the company's full-time agent for the sale and importation of cars, concluding sales contracts in the UK, then Zavok Inc. would be liable to corporation tax on the profits of the agency. The profits of the branch or agency, wherever arising, are chargeable. If the Zavok factory above were to sell cars assembled in the UK to (say) Scandinavia, the branch would thus be liable to corporation tax on the profits of the sales to Scandinavia.

It follows that a non-resident company which does not trade through a branch or agency is not charged to corporation tax; if it does, in fact, trade in the UK (but *not* through a branch or agency) – e.g., by reason of a visiting employee of the overseas resident company concluding contracts in the UK – the profits of this trade, earned by the overseas resident company, will be liable to *income tax* (Ss.6(2) and 11(1), TA 1988). This is one of the rare circumstances in which a company can be liable to income tax on its profits.

As to a trade being conducted in the UK early cases established that if sales contracts were made *outside* the UK between a UK resident purchaser and a non-resident company, then this was trading *with* the UK and no liability to UK tax arose. A trade conducted *in* the UK, liable to corporation tax if conducted through a branch or agency and otherwise to income tax, was a trade where contracts were completed *in* the UK, for example by an agent (profits resulting would be liable to corporation tax) or a visiting employee (profits resulting would be liable to income tax).

The above are the rules of the domestic law. These are superseded by the rules of any double tax convention in any particular case (S.788, TA 1988).

In most cases in practice, a double tax convention will apply and will require study. Generally the provisions of the double tax agreement will have a thrust which is similar in its overall effect to the domestic law.

In the context of the chargeability to corporation tax of profits of a 'branch or agency', the words 'branch or agency' have been superseded by the term 'permanent establishment' in double tax treaties. The general notion is that the profits of a non-resident company will be chargeable only to the extent that they arise to a 'permanent establishment'.

In 1963 the Organisaton for Economic Co-operation and

Development (OECD) adopted a draft double tax convention which has formed the framework of modern UK double tax agreements. In this modern agreement a 'permanent establishment' is defined as follows:

(a) a place of management
(b) a branch
(c) an office
(d) a factory
(e) a workshop
(f) a mine, quarry or other place of extraction of natural resources
(g) a building site or construction or assembly project which exists for more than 12 months.

A permanent establishment also includes an agent (not of independent status) if he has, and habitually exercises, an authority to conclude contracts in the name of the overseas company (but not if his activities are limited to the purchase of goods or merchandise for the enterprise). Various operations are excluded, however, from the definition of a permanent establishment including facilities for storage, display, advertising, purchasing and gathering information.

If the non-resident company intends to establish itself in the UK, the most common choice lies between a branch of the overseas company or a subsidiary of the overseas company. The profits arising to both entities are subject to corporation tax. As to the choice between a branch or corporate structure, this will depend on a range of factors including the domestic tax laws of the non-resident investor, and whether or not the non-resident company has other UK subsidiaries.

The conventional wisdom is that a new UK activity is begun in a branch which is subsequently incorporated as a UK subsidiary of the non-resident parent. In this way any start-up losses experienced by the branch, other things being equal, may be allowed against the profits of the overseas company under the tax rules of the overseas country and also carried forward for set off against the profits of the UK subsidiary (see below). Subsequently any profits of the UK subsidiary will be taxed only in the country of the overseas parent to the extent that dividends are paid.

Any losses in the UK branch are available for carry forward into the UK subsidiary company since the overseas company is ceasing to carry on a trade and another company which it controls begins to carry it on. These are circumstances which bring S.343, TA 1988 (Company reconstructions without change of ownership) into play.

There are not only tax but commercial and financial considerations to be considered when deciding whether a branch or subsidiary company is the appropriate medium for investment. For example, the liability of an overseas company for the debts of a branch will be unlimited where as the liability of an overseas parent for the debts of its UK subsidiary are strictly limited. A branch can be set up with fewer administrative and legal requirements than can a limited company. Again it may be more commercially successful to market a product or activity through a local UK company rather than through what is perceived by the public as a foreign operation. Confidentiality about the operation is best maintained through a branch which discloses details of its operations and profits to only a few persons, including the Inland Revenue, while a UK subsidiary makes public disclosure of its accounts in the normal way. If a non-resident company has other UK subsidiaries it will obtain group relief for any losses only if the new activity is incorporated and the new company is a member of the UK group with a UK holding company; group relief in relation to an overseas company as such – e.g., in relation to a branch – is not possible since the provisions for group relief apply only to companies resident in the United Kingdom (S.413(5), TA 1988).

Finally whereas there are no obstacles as far as tax is concerned in remitting branch profits to its overseas head office, tax issues arise in remitting profits of a UK subsidiary to its overseas parent. Payments of dividends involve payments of ACT in the UK. Certain double tax agreements (but by no means all) provide for a repayment to the overseas company of a part (calculated in accordance with the treaty) of the ACT (or what is the same thing, the tax credit). Payment of a management charge to the overseas parent may be made gross, as can payments for know-how. However, payments of patent royalties and interest generally have to be made under deduction of basic rate tax unless a double tax treaty permits payment gross and the Inspector of Foreign Dividends has granted permission.

7.7 OUTWARD INVESTMENT

Outward investment is the mirror image of inward investment, and many of the considerations discussed above apply to outward investment.

The double tax treaty with the country in which it is proposed to operate will form the framework of reliefs and charges. In all cases, whether or not a treaty is in existence, the commercial, legal and fiscal position overseas will need to be considered.

The profits of an overseas branch of a UK resident company are chargeable to corporation tax under the UK schedules appropriate to each source, which in the case of a trading branch will be principally Schedule D Case I. The computation of profits, relief for capital allowances, etc. will proceed in the normal way, and the profits or losses of the branch being part of a UK company's results will be available for group relief purposes to other UK group members and for deduction of charges. Corporation tax arises on chargeable gains realised on overseas assets of an overseas branch but roll-over relief is available (S.115, CGTA 1979). Roll-over relief is a postponement of tax on capital gains when the proceeds of disposal of most business assets are reinvested in other business assets.

As in the case of investments in the UK, it is often suggested that a UK company should begin with a branch overseas and obtain any loss relief which may be available. It will then, subsequently incorporate.

On the incorporation of an overseas branch capital gains which would otherwise accrue (on the transfer of chargeable assets from the UK company, a legal person, to an overseas subsidiary, a separate legal person) may be postponed in the way set out in S.268A, TA 1970.

When sales of certain assets – including industrial buildings which have obtained capital allowances – are made between, for example, a UK parent company and a UK subsidiary, a number of special rules apply, including the application of open market value as the sale price. This can have the result of creating a substantial *balancing charge* in the hands of the seller and provision is made in respect of UK companies to elect that the special rules do not apply and that, generally, the subsidiary company stands in the shoes of the parent as regards, for example, IBAs and balancing adjustments (Paras.1 and 4, Sched.7, CAA 1968). The elective procedure will not apply where a non-resident company is involved, and as a result balancing charges (particularly in respect of industrial buildings) may arise where a branch is incorporated.

The profits of a foreign subsidiary of a UK company will not, it may be assumed, be subject to corporation tax, because it will be possible to show that the board of the subsidiary meets overseas and that central management and control is overseas. Dividends from the subsidiary will be assessed under Schedule D Case V, and treaty relief or unilateral relief will be available in respect of so-called withholding and underlying taxes (see below).

7.8 DOUBLE TAX RELIEF

As we have seen above, where a UK company trades through a branch overseas the profits of the branch trade will be taxed both in the state of its operations and in the UK. Furthermore when a dividend is paid to a UK parent by an overseas subsidiary a withholding tax may be deducted from the dividend and the gross amount of this dividend taxed under Schedule D Case V in the UK. To provide relief from the effects of profit and income being taxed twice in this way, double tax conventions provide for relief in a variety of ways. A common relief is called *credit relief* where foreign tax charged on the income is deducted from the UK corporation tax charged on the same income.

The amount of the double tax credit relief is limited to the amount of the corporation tax charged on the foreign income (S.797(1), TA 1988). In arriving at the amount of the foreign income, charges and expenses of management may be set off as the company sees fit (and is most advantageous to it) (S.797(3), TA 1988). The corporation tax charge on the foreign income is before deduction of any ACT paid in the AP (S.797(4), TA 1988).

Example 1
Northern Gate Ltd in its AP ended 31 December 1988 has total profits of £800,000. The company paid no charges or dividends in the year ended 31 December 1988, and total profits of £800,000 are made up of UK profits £600,000, foreign profits £200,000. Foreign profits suffered foreign tax of £80,000.

Double tax relief is limited as follows:

	UK (£)	Foreign source (£)	Total (£)
Profits	600,000	200,000	800,000
Corporation tax chargeable:			
£600,000 @ 35%	210,000		210,000
£200,000 @ 35%		70,000	70,000
	210,000	70,000	280,000
Double tax relief restricted to		70,000	70,000
	210,000		210,000
Foreign tax unrelieved is:			
Foreign tax paid			80,000
Relieved			70,000
Unrelieved			10,000

Note particularly that unrelieved foreign tax is *not* available for carry forward for relief in subsequent years.

In the above case, the amount of unrelieved tax is the difference between the higher overseas rate of tax and the lower UK rate of tax. It represents the 'premium' for operating in the overseas country, and there would seem to be no self-evident reason why it should be relieved. On the other hand, circumstances may arise where by reason (for example) of FYAs, no UK tax is payable on overseas profits but foreign tax arises because the overseas country does not operate the same system of accelerated capital allowances as were available in the UK down to 31 March 1986. Since no UK tax is payable there is no tax against which credit relief can be taken, and credit relief is not available in later years when FYAs are not available and consequently UK tax becomes payable. In such circumstances, the appropriate action would have been to disclaim FYAs in order that profits suffer UK tax in the same year as that in which foreign tax is payable.

In other situations where UK losses arise and it is not possible to obtain treaty credit relief for foreign tax paid on overseas profits, the foreign tax may be regarded as an *expense* and increase the amount of UK tax losses. This method of proceeding (treating foreign taxes paid as an expense) antedates treaty credit relief or unilateral credit relief, and gives substantially less relief than does credit relief (tax against tax), which will be taken wherever possible.

The amount of foreign income to be included in total profits for corporation tax is the amount received plus the amount of the foreign tax. The foreign tax on overseas dividends in certain circumstances may include underlying tax on the profits out of which the dividends were paid. 'Underlying tax' is the foreign tax paid by the overseas company on the company profits out of which it has paid dividends. Underlying tax will be included in foreign dividend income where convention relief or unilateral relief (see immediately below) is available in respect of underlying tax.

Where convention relief is not available, S.790, TA 1988 provides what is known as unilateral relief, generally, and in the context of underlying taxes and dividends provides relief for underlying taxes where the UK company controls at least 10% of the voting power of the overseas company paying the dividend. S.799, TA 1988 sets out the statutory provisions concerning the computation of underlying tax.

Example 2

Globo Ltd is a company resident in the UK. In addition to the trade which Globo Ltd conducts in the UK, the company conducts a trade through a branch in an overseas country, Globo Ltd also has a wholly owned overseas subsidiary from which it receives dividends. The double tax convention provides relief for underlying as well as withholding taxes. The results of Globo Ltd for the year ended 31 March 1989 are as follows:

	£	£
Schedule D Case I, UK		500,000
Schedule D Case I, foreign branch		100,000
Foreign tax payable £30,000		
Schedule D Case V, dividend received from subsidiary	50,000	
Less: Withholding tax @ 15%	7,500	42,500

Underlying tax with respect to the dividend computed to be 20%. In June 1988, Globo Ltd paid a dividend of £150,000. The surplus of

ACT brought forward from the year ended 31 March 1988 is
£200,000. Double tax relief is available as follows:

	UK trade (£)	Foreign dividend (£)	Foreign branch trade (£)	Total (£)
Trading income	500,000		100,000	600,000
Dividend income				
£50,000 × $\frac{100}{80}$				
(grossed up for underlying tax)		62,500		62,500
	500,000	62,500	100,000	662,500
Corporation tax @ 35%	175,000	21,875	35,000	231,875
Double tax relief		20,000	30,000	50,000
	175,000	1,875	5,000	181,875
ACT restricted to	125,000	1,875	5,000	131,875
Mainstream corporation tax	50,000	—	—	50,000

Surplus ACT at 31 March 1989:	
Surplus at 31 March 1988	200,000
Paid on dividend June 1988	50,000
	250,000
Applied year ended 31 March 1989	131,875
Surplus at 31 March 1989	118,125

As you see above, the ACT deduction from the corporation tax
liability on the foreign income is restricted to the corporation tax
which remains payable after deduction of double tax relief (£1,875
and £5,000 in Example 2). The amount of the ACT deduction
from the corporation tax chargeable on the UK income is still
restricted to 25% (basic rate of income tax 1988/89) of the UK
taxable income – 25% of £500,000 in Example 2, £125,000.

7.9 CONTROLLED FOREIGN COMPANIES

At the start of the 1980s the Board of the Inland Revenue issued a
consultative document entitled 'Tax Havens and the Corporate

Sector'. In this document, it was stated 'The use of tax havens for tax avoidance companies has shown a marked growth in recent years, and the Government is particularly concerned to counter avoidance of United Kingdom tax by the accumulation of profits and investment income of United Kingdom groups in tax haven subsidiaries'. The paper proposed two things, first that the terms on which a company is regarded as resident should be recast (a consultative paper on residence was issued at the same time) and second that legislation should be introduced which would impose a UK charge to tax on the income and gains of defined companies resident in tax havens. The proposal was that such a UK charge would be apportioned to the overseas companies' corporate shareholder or shareholders – i.e., the UK parent of a tax haven subsidiary.

The legislation to give effect to these proposals was contained in 42 pages of legislation. All of it is highly detailed anti-avoidance legislation, much of which is out of place here.

The legislation applies to UK companies with at least a 10% interest (including the interests of associated or connected persons) in a controlled foreign company and apportions the 'chargeable profits' and 'creditable tax' of the controlled foreign company (CFC) to any UK resident company which is a shareholder. The effect of this is to charge the profits (other than capital gains) of the CFC as if it had been resident in the UK. The apportioned sum is charged to UK corporation tax in the hands of the UK shareholder company, subject to relief for double tax (S.747(2), TA 1988).

A CFC is

(a) resident outside the UK,
(b) controlled by persons resident in the UK, and
(c) subject to a lower level of taxation in the territory in which it is resident (S.747(1), TA 1988).

A 'lower level of taxation' is defined as less than one-half of the corresponding UK tax (S.750(1), TA 1988).

The legislation is not mandatory, and applies only where the Board of Inland Revenue directs (S.747(1), TA 1988).

The government has gone to some lengths to detail the circumstances in which a direction will *not* be given, the object being in a general way to exclude from the effects of the legislation trivial cases, where chargeable profits are less than £20,000; cases where the CFC pursues an 'acceptable' distribution policy (e.g., 50% of available profits of a CFC which is a trading company); cases where the activity of the CFC is exempt – i.e., the CFC has a business establishment and its business affairs are effectively managed in the overseas territory and where other very detailed conditions are satisfied; cases where the CFC has a public quotation – i.e., 35% of the voting power is held by the public and shares are quoted and dealt in on a local stock exchange, and cases where the motive for setting up the CFC or transactions giving rise to a reduction in UK tax was not to reduce UK tax or to divert profits (S.748 and Sched.25, TA 1988).

The intentional effect of these conclusions will be that bona fide commercial investments in tax havens will not be subject to a statutory apportionment.

Question 7

Xan Ltd, a UK resident company manufacturing specialised tools and drills for the mining and oil industries, sells annually £200,000 worth of plant to Norway. In order to meet an increased demand from Norwegian customers it is proposed that Xan Ltd set up a factory in Norway. It is believed that a suitable factory can be purchased for £100,000 and that equipment for the factory will cost a further £90,000. In the first year it is anticipated that the Norwegian operation will make a trading loss of £50,000. It is anticipated that the UK operations of Xan Ltd will also make a loss in that year. However Zax Ltd, a wholly owned UK subsidiary of Xan, is expected to make substantial profits in the same year.

After a time it is expected that Xan Ltd will incorporate its Norwegian operations when they become profitable.

You are required to prepare notes for a preliminary meeting with the managing director of Xan Ltd, setting out the likely taxation consequences of the course of action proposed. What further information might you require?

APPENDIX 1

CORPORATION TAX WORK FORM

Accounting period from .... 19 .... to .... 19.....

	£	£
Schedule D Cases I and II (if a loss, enter 'Nil')		
Less: Losses or charges treated as losses (S.393(1), S.393(9), S.242(5))	....	....
Schedule D Case III		....
Schedule D Case IV and V		....
Schedule D Case IV	....	
Less: Losses (S.396)	....	....
UFII		....
Group interest		....
Building society interest		....
Schedule A		....
Chargeable gains	....	....
Less: Losses	....	....
		....
Less: Trading losses set against profits (S.393(2))	....	
Management expenses	....	....
Less: Charges paid		....
Less: Group relief		....
Profits chargeable to corporation tax		£

TAX CHARGEABLE   £

Relevant financial years (s)

19 ..... at ..... % on £	....
19 ..... at ..... % on £	....
19 ..... at ..... % on £	....
19 ..... at ..... % on £	....

Less: Marginal small companies relief
  (S.13, TA 1988) (restricted if necessary) ....

Less: Double taxation relief (S.797(4), TA 1988) ....

Less ACT (restricted if necessary) ....

Less Income tax set-off ....

     Corporation tax payable ....
     Income tax repayable ....

APPENDIX 2

INDUSTRIAL BUILDINGS: TABLE OF RATES, INITIAL AND ANNUAL ALLOWANCE

Date of expenditure		Rates of allowance	
From	*To*	*Initial* %	*Annual* %
6/4/44	5/4/52	10	2
6/4/52	14/4/53	—	2
15/4/53	6/4/54	10	2
7/4/54	17/2/56	—	2
18/2/56	14/4/58	10	2
15/4/58	7/4/59	15	2
8/4/59	5/11/62	5	2
6/11/62	16/1/66	5	4
17/1/66	5/4/70	15	4
6/4/70	21/3/72	[1]40	4
22/3/72	12/11/74	40	4
13/11/74	10/3/81	50	4
11/3/81	13/3/84	75	4
14/3/84	31/3/85	50	4
1/4/85	31/3/86	25	4
1/4/86	onwards	—	4

[1]30% if not in Development or Intermediate Area, for expenditure between 6 April 1970 and 21 March 1972.

APPENDIX 3

EXAMINATION QUESTIONS 8–13

Question 8

Micro Chip Ltd is a non-close company involved in the distribution of microprocessors. It has an issued share capital of 100,000 ordinary shares of £1 each. The accounts to 31 March 1988 show a profit of £175,000 before tax and appropriations. The profit was arrived at after charging:

	£
Depreciation	27,875
Directors' remuneration	14,000
Legal expenses re sale of field	1,500
Loan interest – gross	2,400
Auditors' remuneration	2,500
Loss on realisation of motor vehicle	500

and after crediting:

	£
Rental income	1,500
Gain on sale of field	12,000
Bad debts recovered	4,000
Dividends received	7,500
Interest on tax repayment	1,000

The fixed asset note to the accounts is as follows:

	Warehouse and land (£)	Plant and machinery (£)	Motor vehicles (£)
Cost at 1 April 1987	150,000	100,000	25,000
Additions	—	25,000	10,000
Disposals	(20,000)	—	(4,093)
Cost at 31 March 1988	130,000	125,000	30,907
Accumulated depreciation at 1 April 1987	15,000	45,000	15,000
Eliminated in respect of disposals	—	—	(1,093)
Charge for year	7,500	16,000	4,375

Accumulated depreciation at 31 March 1988	22,500	61,000	18,282
Net book value at 31 March 1988	107,500	64,000	12,625

Notes:

1. The tax WDV of the car pool brought forward at 1 April 1987 was £10,000. The tax WDV of the general pool at 1 April 1987 was Nil. The motor vehicle disposed of was the managing director's Rover bought second-hand two years ago and replaced in October 1987 with a new one costing £10,000.
2. The loan interest was unpaid at the year end although outstanding loan interest at 31 March 1987 of £2,250 net was paid during the year on 15 November 1987.
3. A field adjoining the warehouse which was acquired in December 1972 was sold in September 1987 for £32,000 (ignore indexation).
4. A general provision for bad debts of £10,000 has been made in the accounts.
5. Miscellaneous expenses include:

	£
Staff party	1,250
Entertaining – foreign	500
– home	750
Interest on overdue tax	70

6. The dividend of £7,500 exclusive of tax credit was received on 4 June 1987.
7. Micro Chip Ltd paid a dividend for 1987 of 15p per share on 30 April 1987. Assume the following:

Corporation tax – normal	35%
Corporation tax – small company	25%
Marginal small company relief – profits between £100,000 and £500,000	
Fraction	1/50
ACT	1/3
Income tax (%)	25

Required:

1. Set out the information which requires to be included in the returns under Sched.13 and Sched.16 (Forms CT61) for the year, detailing the return periods and the amount and date of payment of tax.
2. Calculate the corporation tax payable for the AP ended 31 March 1988.

   (*The Institute of Chartered Accountants of Scotland, updated and amended*).

Question 9

The undernoted are the agreed results of 5 companies for the year ended
31 December 1988:

	One Ltd (£)	Two Ltd (£)	Three Ltd (£)	Four Ltd (£)	Five Ltd (£)
Case I profit/(loss)	30,000	(60,000)	(82,000)	666,000	100,000
Case III	10,000	—	2,000	10,000	—
Schedule A surplus/ (deficit)	5,000	—	—	(1,000)	—
Chargeable gain/(loss)	(100,000)	—	—	60,000	—
Non-trading charges paid (gross)	—	—	30,000	20,000	—

The 5 companies are connected as follows:

1. One Ltd owns 100% of Two Ltd and 60% of Three Ltd.
2. Two Ltd owns 80% of Four Ltd.
3. Three Ltd owns 100% of Five Ltd.

The following additional information has been ascertained:

(a) The 100% shareholding in Five Ltd was acquired by Three Ltd
on 1 July 1988.
(b) One Ltd paid a dividend of £60,000 on 1 November 1988 and
remitted the appropriate ACT on 14 January 1989.

Assume the following:

Corporation tax rate (%)	35
ACT	1/3
Income tax rate (%)	25

Required:

1. Determine which of the above companies form a group for the
purposes of group relief in the context of corporation tax.
2. Compute the corporation tax liabilities, if any, for each of the 5
companies for the year to 31 December 1988, on the basis that the
desired aim is for the 5 companies in aggregate to pay the minimum
amount of taxation.
3. State what unutilised losses and other reliefs are available for carry
forward at 31 December 1988.

(*The Institute of Chartered Accountants of Scotland updated and
amended*).

Question 10

Itchen Ltd is a manufacturing company with an issued capital of £575,000 in ordinary shares of £1. Since 1969 the company has owned 60,000 ordinary shares of £1 each in Easton Ltd, which has an issued capital of 75,000 such shares.

On 1 April 1986 Itchen Ltd acquired the whole issued capital of Avington Ltd, which consists of 18,000 ordinary shares of £1 each. Avington Ltd has been trading at a loss since 1983, but it is expected that the company will break even in the year ended 30 September 1987 and become profitable thereafter.

Information relating to each company for the accounting period ended 30 September 1986 is shown below:

Itchen Ltd
The profit and loss account for the year ended 30 September 1986 showed a trading profit of £66,456, surplus on sale of freehold factory £97,000 and investment income £17,494. Further detail is given below.

(1) Expenses charged in arriving at trading profit include the following:

	£
Directors' remuneration	74,250
Depreciation	9,100
Patent royalties (gross)	12,460

(2) The charge for patent royalties is made up as follows:

	£
Paid 30 November 1985	6,150
Paid 31 May 1986	5,420
Accrued at 30 September 1986	3,830
Less: accrued at 1 October 1985	(2,940)
	12,460

(3) The surplus on sale of freehold factory is made up as follows:

	Land (£)	Buildings (£)	Total (£)
Proceeds in June 1986	35,000	125,000	160,000
Cost in 1970	11,000	52,000	63,000
	24,000	73,000	97,000

The factory had been built for Itchen Ltd and had been used continuously for industrial purposes, the residual value for IBA purposes being £10,920 on 1 October 1985.

On 8 March 1986, Itchen Ltd occupied a new factory built on land which it had bought for £27,500 in June 1984. The cost of construction was £188,000; in accordance with the terms of the contract, a progress payment of £50,000 had been made in July 1985 and the balance of £138,000 was paid in March 1986.

All possible allowances and reliefs have been claimed for both
factories.
(4) There are no capital allowances on plant, which is all leased.
(5) Investment income consists of the following items:

	£
Dividend from Easton Ltd (paid under a group election to pay dividends without accounting for ACT)	6,600
Dividends from other UK companies (including tax credit)	5,184
Interest on government securities (gross)	4,000
Bank interest	1,710
	17,494

The investment income was received during the following periods:

Quarter ended	31 December 1985 (£)	31 March 1986 (£)	30 June 1986 (£)	30 September 1986 (£)
Group dividend	—	6,600	—	—
Other dividends	3,264	—	—	1,920
Interest on government securities	—	1,080	1,320	1,600
Bank interest	430	740	540	—

None of this income was received between 1 April and 5 April 1986.
(6) In January 1986 Itchen Ltd paid a dividend of 8% for the year ended
30 September 1985.

Easton Ltd
The Schedule D Case I profit of Easton Ltd for the year ended
30 September 1986 has been agreed at £26,820. The company had no
other income and paid no charges; its only investment was sold in
November 1985, the chargeable gain (before the reduction applicable to
companies) being £5,880.
In January 1986 Easton Ltd paid a dividend of 11% for the year ended
30 September 1985.

Avington Ltd
Avington Ltd had made up accounts to 31 January 1986 before the
acquisition by Itchen Ltd; unrelieved trading losses carried forward at that
date were £31,100.
The next accounts were made up for the 8 months ended 30 September
1986 and a Schedule D Case I loss of £71,200 has been agreed. The
company had no other source of income and paid no charges; it last paid a
dividend in 1983.

Required:

(a) Show how and when Itchen Ltd should account to the Inland

Revenue for ACT and income tax for the year ended
30 September 1986 (**5 marks**).
(b) Calculate the mainstream corporation tax payable by Itchen Ltd
and Easton Ltd for the year ended 30 September 1986, before
considering any relief for amounts surrendered by Avington Ltd
(**13 marks**).
(c) List the ways in which relief may be obtained for the loss of
Avington Ltd for the 8 months ended 30 September 1986,
indicating the advantages and disadvantages of each and
suggesting which method should be used (**9 marks**).

(**27 marks**)

The Institute of Chartered Accountants in England and Wales).

Question 11

Dean Ltd, which has one associated company, has carried on a manufacturing business since 1976 and has always made up accounts to 30 June in
each year. For commercial reasons, the directors have this year changed
the accounting reference date to 31 March. The accounts for the 9 months
ended 31 March 1988 show the following:

	£
Trading profit	3,386
Building society interest received (gross)	10,450
Dividends received from UK companies (including tax credits)	5,800
Profit on disposal of freehold factory building	55,608
Interest paid on 10% debentures (gross)	(6,070)
Profit before taxation	69,174

The trading profit is after charging (crediting) the following items:

	£
Leasing charges of car (original cost £10,375)	3,018
Leasing charges of car (original cost £7,000)	2,237
Political donations	100
Bad and doubtful debts	4,158
Legal fees	5,089
Depreciation	24,685
Profit on disposal of plant and machinery	(220)
Directors' remuneration	41,600
Auditors' remuneration	7,850

The bad and doubtful debts provision at 1 July 1987 comprised specific provisions of £6,975 and a general provision of £11,240. In the 9 months ended 31 March 1987, £2,475 of the opening specific provisions, as well as £3,158 of bad debts arising in the period, were written off; there were no other changes in specific provisions in that period but the general provision was increased by £1,000 at 31 March 1988.

The legal fees comprised £424 relating to the renewal of an existing short lease on a sales office, £3,720 relating to the disposal of the freehold factory building, and £945 relating to the acquisition of a new short lease on land used for storage purposes.

For capital allowances purposes, the pool WDV was nil at 1 July 1987. Additions in the period comprised 2 new commercial delivery vehicles costing £11,380 each in September 1987 and 2 motor cars costing £7,270 each in February 1987. The only disposal was that of a commercial delivery vehicle sold for less than cost, which realised £500 in September 1987.

Until concentration of all manufacturing in the Swindon factory in September 1987 the company had two freehold factories, the factory at Swindon purchased in July 1978 for £230,000 (including land costing £40,000) and another at Bristol purchased in July 1980 for £130,000 (including land costing £38,000). In the Swindon factory offices represent 30%, a canteen 12.5% and manufacturing space 57.5%; the Bristol factory was 100% manufacturing. The IA on both purchases was at the rate of 50%. On moving all production into the Swindon factory in September 1987 the Bristol factory was sold in the same month for £200,280. No election for 31 March 1982 market value has been made for the purpose of the indexation allowance. The company did not purchase any assets which would rank for rollover relief in the 9 months ended 31 March 1988 or the preceding AP, and it is not envisaged that any will be purchased in the foreseeable future.

At 1 July 1987, the company had surplus ACT of £7,614 and agreed trading losses of £98,878 brought forward.

The company paid the following dividends on its 200,000 ordinary shares of £1 each:

> 6 November 1987 Interim dividend for the 9 months ended 31 March 1987 of 7.3p per share
> 1 September 1988 Final dividend for the 9 months ended 31 March 1987 of 3p per share

Requirements:

(a) Calculate the mainstream corporation tax payable by Dean Ltd for the 9 months ended 31 March 1988 on the assumption that all available reliefs and allowances are claimed as early as possible (**17 marks**).

(b) On the same basis as in (a), calculate the mainsteam corporation tax payable if the Schedule D Case I profits for the 9 months ended 31 March 1988 were to be increased by £150,000 (**3 marks**).
(c) State what IBAs will be given to, or charges made on, the purchaser of the Bristol factory in each of the following circumstances:
  (i) It is used by him continuously for manufacturing purposes for the foreseeable future.
  (ii) It is used by him for 2 years for manufacturing purposes, then left empty for 2 years and then again used for manufacturing purposes for 2 years, until sold by him (**3 marks**).

(**23 marks**)

Note:

The indexation factor March 1982 to September 1987 is 28.9.

(*The Institute of Chartered Accountants in England and Wales, PE1 examinations, Elements of Taxation, November 1985, updated and amended*).

Question 12

Stratagem Ltd is a close company incorporated in 1981 with its accounts being made up to 31 March each year. For its AP ended 31 March 1988 its results are summarised below:

	£
Trading income (before capital allowances)	546,000
Schedule A income	12,500
Schedule D Case III income	640
Debenture interest paid (gross)	6,000
Dividend from a UK company (excluding tax credit)	730

The following information is also available:

(i) The WDVs of fixed assets at 1 April 1987 for capital allowance purposes were:

Plant and machinery (pool)	44,800
Cars (3)	15,750
Car (cost £12,100 February 1987)	10,100

During the year under consideration, the company sold a piece of machinery costing £5,000 for £3,100 and paid £6,500 for a car after receiving a trade-in allowance of £2,250 for one of its existing cars having a WDV value of less than £8,000.
(ii) On 4 July 1987 it sold its entire holding of 5,000 shares in Tactic Plc for £5,200; the shares were purchased in May 1983 for £5,450.

(iii) Dividends paid or proposed are:

Date of payment	Amount (£)	AP
2 August 1987	146,000	Year ended 31 March 1987
14 November 1987	73,000	Year ended 31 March 1988
10 August 1988	126,000	Year ended 31 March 1988

(iv) Debenture interest due but unpaid at 31 March 1988 amounted to £2,000 (gross).

(v) During the year a major shareholder, not a director, received a benefit-in-kind from the company amounting to £365.

Required:

(a) Compute the mainstream corporation tax payable by Stratagem Ltd for the AP to 31 March 1988, assuming any available 'set-offs' are claimed, and calculate any losses that may be carried forward (**18 marks**).

(b) Calculate the company's maximum relevant income (**9 marks**).

(**27 marks**)

(*Institute of Chartered Secretaries and Administrators, updated and amended*).

Note:

The indexation factor on the disposal of the shares in Tactic Plc is 0.225.

Question 13

(a) Q Ltd, which commenced to trade on 1 December 1986, is a wholly owned subsidiary of T Ltd. Trading results are as follows:

	Q Ltd (£)	T Ltd (£)
Year to 30 November 1986		
Trading profit/(loss)		(5,000)
Year to 30 November 1987		
Trading profit/(loss)	(12,000)	10,000
Bank interest received	—	5,000
Debenture interest (gross) paid	—	2,000
Year to 30 November 1988		
Trading profit/(loss)	(5,000)	(10,000)
Bank interest received	—	5,000
Debenture interest (gross) paid	—	2,000

Required:
Illustrate how loss relief is claimed, and why you make your particular form of claim in these circumstances. Explain how unrelieved losses and charges may be dealt with.

(b) The issued share capital of Z Ltd is 80,000 £1 ordinary shares. 48,000 are owned by A Ltd, 24,000 by B Ltd and 8,000 by C Ltd. Trading results of all companies, which are resident in the UK for the year to 30 June 1988 are:

	£
Z Ltd profit	50,000
A Ltd profit	40,000
B Ltd loss	(60,000)
C Ltd profit	10,000

Explain fully how, and in what conditions, B Ltd's loss may be relieved.

(*Chartered Association of Certified Accountants, updated*).

APPENDIX 4

SOLUTIONS TO QUESTIONS 1–13

Question 1

Exer Sighs Ltd
Corporation Tax Computation
Year ended 31 March 1988

1. Schedule D Case I computation

	£	£
Profit before tax		77,075
Add: Depreciation		11,625
Loss on sale of machine		650
Charges		7,000
		96,350
Deduct: FII	2,000	
Deposit account interest	300	
Debenture interest	6,200	
Building society interest	500	9,000
		87,350
Deduct: Capital allowances		26,350
Schedule D Case I profit		61,000

2. Corporation tax computations

	£	£
Schedule D Case I profit		61,000
Schedule D Case III		300
UFII		6,200
Building society interest		
£500 × $\dfrac{100}{73}$		685
Chargeable gain		32,000
		100,185
Less: Deed of covenant	2,000	
Loan interest	2,500	
		4,500
Profits chargeable to corporation tax		95,685

214

Corporation tax payable: £95,685 × 27%	25,834.95
Deduct: Income tax suffered £1,859 − £1,215	644.00
Corporation tax payable by 1 January 1989	£25,190.95

Notes to computation:

1. The total of the 'other income', £9,000, is deducted in arriving at the Schedule D Case I profit, since this is not trading income. Items (b), (c) and (d) are then included in the corporation tax computation under the relevant headings. FII is not included in the computation of profits chargeable to corporation tax.

2. Charges of £7,000 are included in the profit and loss account and are added back in arriving at the Schedule D Case I profit. Note that only £4,500 may be deducted in the corporation tax computation. The payment of £2,500 due on 31 March was not paid until after the end of the AP.

3. For small company relief purposes, the 'profits' of Exer Sighs Ltd are calculated as follows:

	£
Profits chargeable to corporation tax	95,685
Add: FII	2,000
'Profits'	97,685

Since the profits are less than £100,000 the 'income' will be charged to tax at the small company rate of 27%.

4. The company has suffered income tax of £1,674 by deduction at source from the debenture interest. During the year the company deducted income tax of £1,215 from the charges paid. The income tax deducted will have been set off against the income tax suffered, and this will be shown on the forms CT 61 submitted during the 12 months to 31 March 1988. The balance of income tax suffered on the UFII for which the company has not obtained relief is £459. In addition, the company is deemed to have suffered income tax of £185 by deduction at source from the building society interest. There will thus be a deduction of £644 from the corporation tax liability.

5. Although the company was trading before 1965, it is not necessary to apply the transitional provisions of Sched.30 para.(1), TA 1988. This is because tax on the company's 1965/66 assessment, for which the basis period was the AP ended 31 March 1965, was due for payment on 1 January 1966, exactly 9 months after the company's year end.

Question 2

Davy Jones Ltd

1. Industrial buildings allowance

AP ended 31 March 1988

		£
Qualifying expenditure		
Total cost		142,000
Less: Cost of land and		
relevant legal fees		21,000
Qualifying expenditure		£121,000

Years ended	Residue 31 March 1987 (£)	Expenditure AP 31 March 1988 (£)	WDA (£)	Residue 31 March 1988 (£)
1988		121,000	4,840	116,160
1981	462		84	378
1976	256		256	—
1970	1,118		344	774
1959	4,736		296	4,440
IBA			5,820	

Notes:
  (i) All the expenditure qualifies for IBA (other than the cost of land, etc.) by reason of being a factory used in a qualifying trade or welfare premises (canteen and kitchen, etc.) or offices directly related to production (drawing office and works manager's office). A storeroom in the context of a manufacturing company qualifies where the store is of raw materials or of finished goods.
  (ii) The WDA in respect of expenditure from · 6 April 1946 to 5 November 1962 (inclusive dates) is at 2%. Thereafter it is 4%.
  (iii) The amount of an annual WDA cannot exceed the amount of the 'residue'.

2. Notes for meeting with accountant
  (a) The estimated £400,000 will require to be analysed between the sale price of the industrial buildings and the sale price of the land.
  (b) Since it seems likely that both land and buildings will be sold for more than cost, a *chargeable gain* will arise.
  (c) The possibility of rolling-over the chargeable gain into group acquisitions of replacement and other business assets will require to be considered. In this regard acquisitions 1 year before disposal and 3 years after disposal are in point. What acquisitions have been made or projected?

(d) The allocation between land and buildings should be agreed in due course between Davy Jones Ltd and the purchaser.
(e) The sale price of the buildings only will require to be apportioned between the different expenditures in each AP. This might be done in proportion to cost but some other manner of apportionment might be appropriate. In particular, are the costs and residues the only expenditure on this factory? There may be expenditures many years ago which do not enter into the IBA computations which are relevant to the calculation of balancing adjustments.
(f) Balancing adjustments will arise in respect of each year's expenditure. These are likely to be balancing charges (limited to allowances given) treated as trading income in the AP of sale.
(g) No allowances (i.e., WDAs) will be granted in the AP of sale.
(h) No balancing adjustment is necessary 50 years after a building (or part of a building) came into use if expenditure was incurred before 6 November 1962 (25 years if the expenditure is after 5 November 1962).
(i) Has the factory been used as an industrial building throughout its ownership by Davy Jones Ltd; in particular were there periods of time during which it was in use otherwise than as an industrial building? In the latter case, notional allowances will be deducted in arriving at the residue of expenditure before sale. Any balancing charge will be restricted to allowances actually granted against profits.

Question 3

Vibrations Ltd

Liability under Sched.13, TA 1988

	£	£
Return period 30 June 1987		
10 April 1987 Dividend received		1,460
Add: Tax credit at 27/73		540
FII carried forward		2,000
Return period ended 30 September 1987		
1 July 1987 Dividend paid		5,475
Add: ACT		2,025
Franked payment		7,500
Less FII brought forward		2,000
		5,500

ACT payable (by 14 October 1987)
£5,500 × 27% = £1,485

Return period ended
  31 December 1987
10 October 1987 Dividend received   3,285
              Add: Tax credit
                  at 27/73   1,215
                                                      ──────
                  FII   4,500
                                                      ──────
              Total franked   7,500
              payments to date
              Less: Total FII
                  to date:
                  10 April 1987   2,000
                  10 October 1987   4,500
                                      ──────   6,500
                                                      ──────
                  Excess of franked
                    payments over
                    FII   1,000
                                                      ──────
                  ACT paid to date   1,485
              Less: ACT due
                  (1,000 × 27%)   270
                                                      ──────
              Repayment to be
                  made by
                  Collector of
                  Taxes
                                                       1,215
                                                      ──────
Return period ended 31 March 1988
1 January 1988   Dividend paid   5,475
22 February 1988 Dividend paid   29,200
                                                      ──────
                                                      34,675
                  Add: ACT at   12,825
                      27/73
                                                      ──────
                  Franked payments   47,500
                                                      ──────

ACT payable £47,500 × 27% = £12,825

Question 4

Machinations Ltd

Corporation tax computations

Years ended	31 March 1986 (£)	31 March 1987 (£)	31 March 1988 (£)	31 March 1989 (£)
Trading profit (loss)	16,000	3,200	(15,000)	22,400
Capital allowances	(9,360)	(900)	(7,350)	(320)
Schedule D Case I	6,640	2,300	(Note 1)	22,080
Less:				
Losses b/f (S.393(1))				(9,360)*
Charges b/f (S.393(9))				(6,200)*
UFII	1,500	4,000	4,000	4,000
Schedule A	720	720	720	720
Chargeable gain less				
capital loss b/f			1,250	
	8,860	7,020	5,970	11,240
Less:				
Loss relief (S.393(2))				
ICTA 1988	—	(7,020)	(5,970)	—
	8,860	—	—	11,240
Less:				
Charges	(1,500)	—	—	(3,600)
Profits chargeable	7,360	—	—	7,640
Corporation tax @ 35%	2,576	—	—	2,674
Less:				
Income tax	—	—	—	(100)
	2,576	—	—	2,574
Income tax repayable	—	(100)	(100)	—
Trade charges b/f	—		3,100	6,200
Trade charges unused/(used)	—	3,100	3,100	(6,200)
Trade charges c/f (S.393(9))	—	3,100	6,200	Nil

* See Note 2.

Notes:
1. The total loss available for relief in the year ended 31 March 1988 is:

	£
Trading loss	15,000
WDA	7,350
	22,350

This loss is utilised as follows:

		£
Loss		22,350
Less: Used in year ended 31 March 1988		(5,970)
Less: Carried back to year ended		
	31 March 1987	(7,020)
Less: Carried forward to year ended		
	31 March 1989	(9,360)
		—

2. Note that trade charges unutilised in 1987 and 1988, £6,200, are carried forward to 1989 and are set off together with the loss carried forward of £9,360 against the Schedule D Case I profit in 1989.
3. Note that the non-trade charges in 1987 and 1988 remain unutilised.
4. Note that in 1987, 1988 and 1989 UFII received by the company (under deduction of tax) exceeds the charges paid. There is therefore an excess of income tax suffered on the UFII over income tax deducted from charges. This excess is repayable by the Inland Revenue to the company in 1987 and 1988, and deductible from corporation tax payable in 1989.

Question 5

1. Group income
S.247, TA 1988 provides that in certain circumstances dividends may be paid by one company within a group to another company within the same group, without accounting for ACT. In the hands of the company receiving the dividend, this income is classified as group income. A joint election must be made by the company receiving the dividend and the company paying the dividend and will apply where:

(i) the company paying the dividend is a 51% subsidiary of the recipient company (i.e., the parent company owns more than 51% of the ordinary share capital of the other); or
(ii) the company paying the dividend is a 51% subsidiary of another UK resident company of which the recipient company is also a 51% subsidiary.

Group income is not included in the profits of the recipient company chargeable to corporation tax.

Group relief
The provisions relating to group relief (Ss.402–413) enable a company which is a member of a 75% group to surrender trading losses, excess charges, management expenses and certain capital allowances to other companies within the same group. For these purposes, a 75% group consists of a parent company and any company of which the parent owns 75% or more of the ordinary share capital. In addition, the parent must be entitled to not less than 75% of the profits

available for distribution to equity holders and to not less than 75% of the subsidiary's assets available to equity holders on a notional winding up.

A company which has incurred trading losses or excess charges, etc. may surrender the whole of the amount available to one company or it may apportion the relief between a number of claimant companies.

Where, however, the AP of the surrendering company does not coincide with that of the claimant company it is necessary to *apportion* the profits of the claimant company and the losses of the surrendering company in order to ensure that relief is given only for the period common to both the surrendering and the claimant companies' APs. Likewise where a company joins or leaves a group, apportionment of profits and losses will be necessary in order that relief should be given only for the period during which both companies are members of the same group.

2. *Corporation tax liabilities*

	£	£
(a) *H Ltd*		
Year ended 31 December 1989		
Case I loss	15,000	
Charges	10,000	
Total available for surrender	25,000	25,000
Allowable capital loss carried forward £5,000		
(b) *M Ltd*		
Year ended 31 December 1989		
Case I profit	20,000	
Chargeable gains	3,000	
Total profits	23,000	23,000
Less: Group relief from H Ltd	23,000	
Profits chargeable	Nil	
		2,000
(c) *T Ltd*		
Year ended 31 December 1989		
Case I profits	100,000	
Less: Loss brought forward (S.393(1))	100,000	
	Nil	
Chargeable gains	30,000	
	30,000	
Less: Charges	30,000	
Profits chargeable	Nil	
Loss carried forward (S.393(1)) £25,000		

Charges available to carry forward £10,000 (assuming charges are incurred wholly and exclusively for the purposes of the trade).

Notes:
(1) The balance of charges of £10,000 is not available for surrender under the provisions of S.403(7). This section permits relief only for charges which exceed the profits for an AP *before* deducting losses or allowances brought forward or carried back from any other AP.
(2) T Ltd has paid ACT of £18,750, calculated as follows:

	£
Dividend paid	60,000
Add: ACT	20,000
Franked payment	80,000
Less: FII	5,000
	75,000

ACT payable: £75,000 × 25% = £18,750

All or part of this ACT may be surrendered to D Ltd. The balance then left in T Ltd may be carried forward, or carried back and set against the corporation tax payable in respect of income of APs commencing within the previous 6 years.

(d) *D Ltd*

Year ended 31 December 1989

Case I profit	10,000
Chargeable gain	3,000
Profits chargeable	13,000

Corporation tax payable:

£13,000 × 35%	4,550
Less: ACT surrendered by T Ltd	3,250
Mainstream CRT payable	1,300

3. *Unutilised losses available for carry forward*

(a) *H Ltd*	£
S.393(1) loss = £25,000 − £23,000	2,000
Capital loss	5,000
(b) M Ltd	Nil
(c) T Ltd	
S.393(1) loss	25,000
Charges (assumed to be trade charges)	10.000
ACT £18,750 − £3,250	15,500

Note that D Ltd is not entitled to claim group relief for the losses of H Ltd because the former is not within the 75% group comprising T Ltd, H Ltd and M Ltd.

Question 6

Mortality Ltd
Maximum Relevant Income Computation
Year ended 31 March 1989
Investment Income

	Trading income (£)	Estate income (£)	FII (£)	UFII (£)	Schedule D Case III (£)	Total (£)
Income	200,000	44,000	75,000	30,000	12,000	361,000
charges				10,000		10,000
	200,000	44,000	75,000	20,000	12,000	351,000
Corporation tax @ 34.1754% (see Note)	68,351	15,037		6,835	4,101	94,324
Distributable income	131,649	28,963	75,000	13,165	7,899	256,676
Less: Trading income	131,649					(131,649)
Abatement 10% of estate or trading or £3,000 if less				3,000		(3,000)
No abatement of estate income since aggregate of estate and trading income in excess of £75,000						
Total						122,027
Estate income		28,963				28,963
Distributable investment income			75,000	10,165	7,899	93,064
Total						122,027

	£
Maximum relevant income:	
50% Estate income (50% × £28,963)	14,482
100% Distributable investment income	93,064
	107,546

Note:

Small company rate	£
Profits:	
Profits chargeable	276,000
Add: FII	100,000
Profits for small company rate	376,000
Corporation tax payable £276,000 at 35%	96,600

Less: Marginal relief

$$\frac{1}{40}(M - P) \times \frac{I}{P}$$

$$\frac{1}{40}\,£(500,000 - 376,000) \times £\left(\frac{276,000}{376,000}\right)$$

2,276

94,324

Equivalent to 34.1754% of profits chargeable

Question 7

Notes for preliminary meeting with Managing Director of Xan Ltd

1. Setting up a factory in Norway will be to set up a branch of Xan Ltd in Norway, and the results of the branch will be governed by the rules of corporation tax.
2. IBA will be available in respect of the Norwegian factory. The normal rules about IBA apply (WDA of 4% of cost).
3. Normal rules about plant or machinery allowances also apply to expenditure on plant for the Norwegian factory.
4. The amount of the loss will be computed in accordance with corporation tax provisions. Together with the anticipated loss of Xan Ltd in the UK the loss may be surrendered by way of group relief to Zax Ltd.
5. On incorporation of the Norwegian branch, the capital allowances previously granted to Xan Ltd may be clawed back by way of balancing charges because the disposal value will be market value.
6. If shares are exchanged by the Norwegian company for the branch trade, any capital gains arising on the disposal of buildings and goodwill from Xan Ltd to the Norwegian company can be postponed in terms of S.268A, TA 1970.
7. It is assumed that the proposed company will be incorporated in Norway and that the directors will meet in Norway and that central control and management on a day-to-day basis will be there, and that accordingly the company will be resident in Norway.
8. The Norwegian company will be subject to Norwegian tax on the basis of the assumption in 7 above. The UK company Xan Ltd will be liable to corporation tax under Schedule D Case V and Schedule D Case IV on dividends and interest received from the Norwegian company.
9. Double tax convention relief will be available on dividends, etc. from the Norwegian company. There is a limit on the amount of this relief which is the UK corporation tax on the foreign income.
10. No group relief will be possible for any losses the Norwegian company may make, nor can the Norwegian company set off losses of its UK parent or UK fellow subsidiaries against any profits it makes.
11. Further matters to be considered include:
    (a) How is the Norwegian company to be financed, locally or from the UK?

(b) Will there be a management charge from Xan Ltd to the Norwegian company?

(c) What are the terms of the UK–Norway double tax treaty?

(d) What sources of local information are available to the company and yourself?

Question 8

Micro Chip Ltd

. *Sched.13*

Return period 1 April 1987 to 30 June 1987		£	£
30 April 1987	Distribution made		15,000
	Add: ACT at 1/3		5,000
	Franked payment		20,000
	Less: FII		
	Dividend received	7,500	
	Plus Tax credit	2,500	
			10,000
	Excess of franked payment over FII		10,000
	ACT payable by 14 July 1987 10,000 × 25%		2,500

Sched.16

Return period 1 October 1987 to 31 December 1987		£
15 November 1987	Loan interest payable	3,000
	Less: income tax deducted	750
	Net payment	2,250

Tax payable to Collector of Taxes: £750 by 14 January 1988

Year ended 31 March 1988

(a) Case I computation

	£	£
Profit per profit and loss account		175,000
Add: Depreciation		27,875
Legal expenses		1,500
Loan interest		2,400
Loss on car		500
General provision for bad debts		10,000

Miscellaneous expenses:		
Entertaining, home		75(
Interest on overdue tax		7(
		218,09:
Less: Rental income	1,500	
Gain on sale of field	12,000	
Dividend received	·7,500	
Interest on tax repayment	1,000	22,00(
		196,09.
Less: Capital allowances		10,12.
Case I profit		185,97(

(b) *Capital allowances computation*

	General pool (£)	Car pool (£)	Expensive car (£)	Allowance (£)
WDV brought forward	—	10,000	—	
Additions	25,000		10,000	
Disposal proceeds (see Note)		(2,500)		
	25,000	7,500	10,000	
WDA @ 25%	6,250	1,875	2,000	10,12.
WDV carried forward	18,750	5,625	8,000	
Total allowances				10,12.

Note:

	£
Proceeds of sale of car	2,500
Loss per the accounts	500
Net book value when sold	3,000
Accumulated depreciation per the accounts	1,093
Original cost (less than £8,000)	4,093

(c) *Corporation tax computation*

Year ended 31 March 1988	£	£	£
Schedule D Case I			185,97(
Schedule A			1,50(
Chargeable gain: proceeds		32,000	
Less: Cost	20,000		
Expenses	1,500	21,500	10,50(
			197,97(

Less: Charges during year:

$£2,250 \times \dfrac{100}{75}$ 3,000

Profits chargeable to corporation tax	194,970

Corporation tax payable: £
£194,970 × 35%   68,239

Less: Marginal small companies relief:

$$\dfrac{1}{50} \times \left[(500,000 - 194,970) \times \dfrac{194,970}{204,970} \right] \quad 5,803$$

ACT   2,500

    8,303

Corporation tax payable   59,936

Question 9

1. For the purposes of group relief given under the provisions of S.402, TA 1988 a group of companies comprises a parent company and all subsidiaries in which that parent owns, either directly or indirectly, 75% or more of the ordinary share capital.
   There are thus two groups of companies in this question, namely:
   (a) a group comprising One Ltd, Two Ltd and Four Ltd; and
   (b) a group comprising Three Ltd and Five Ltd (with effect from 1 July 1988).

2. *Corporation tax liabilities*
   (a) *Two Ltd*
   Corporation tax computation

Year ended 31 December 1988	£
Schedule D Case I profit	Nil
Loss available for surrender (S.403, TA 1988)	60,000

   (b) *One Ltd*
   Corporation tax computation

Year ended 31 December 1988	£
Schedule D Case I	30,000
Schedule D Case III	10,000
Schedule A	5,000
Profits chargeable to corporation tax	45,000
Corporation tax payable: £45,000 × 35%	15,750

   Less: ACT:
   £60,000 × 1/3 = £20,000

ACT set-off restricted to £45,000 × 25%	11,250
Mainstream corporation tax payable	4,500

ACT available to surrender to Four Ltd
(S.240, TA 1988):

	£
ACT payable	20,000
Less: ACT set-off	11,250
Available to surrender	8,750

(c) *Four Ltd*
Corporation tax computation
Year ended 31 December 1988

	£
Schedule D Case I	660,000
Schedule D Case III	10,000
Chargeable gain	60,000
	730,000
Less: Charges	20,000
	710,000
Less: Group relief surrendered by Two Ltd	60,000
	650,000
Corporation tax payable: 650,000 × 35%	227,500
Less: ACT surrendered by One Ltd	8,750
Mainstream corporation tax	218,750

(d) *Three Ltd*
Corporation tax computation
Year ended 31 December 1988

	£
Schedule D Case I	Nil
Schedule D Case III	2,000
	2,000
Less: Charges	2,000
	Nil

	£
Group relief available for surrender	
Trading loss	82,000
Charges unutilised (S.403(7)):	
£30,000 − £2,000	28,000
Available to surrender	110,000

(e) *Five Ltd*
Corporation tax computation
Year ended 31 December 1988

	£
Schedule D Case I profit	100,000
Less: Group relief surrendered (S.409(2))	50,000
Profits chargeable to corporation tax	50,000
Corporation tax payable: £50,000 × 35%	17,500

Note:

Five Ltd did not become a subsidiary of Three Ltd until 1 July 1988 and therefore the provisions of S.409(2) apply: The maximum loss that can be surrendered by Three Ltd is £110,000 × 6/12 = £55,000

The maximum profits of Five Ltd against which group relief may be allowed is

£100,000 × 6/12 = £50,000

The group relief surrendered to Five Ltd will be taken to comprise:

	£
Charges	14,000
Loss	36,000
	50,000

3. *Unutilised losses and reliefs*

One Ltd – allowable capital loss of £100,000 available to carry forward
Three Ltd – trading loss available for carry forward:

	£
Trading loss	82,000
Less: Surrendered to Five Ltd	36,000
Loss to carry forward (S.393(1))	46,000

Note that the balance of non-trade charges unutilised *may not* be carried forward

Four Ltd – Schedule A deficit to be carried forward and set against future rents £1,000.

Question 10

Itchen Ltd

AP ended 30 September 1986
    (a)(i) *ACT accounting*
        Return quarter ended 31 December 1985

	£
FII received	3,264

FII carried forward to next return period

Note:
No return required for this return period but see income tax accounting below.

Return quarter ended 31 March 1986	£	£
FII brought forward from previous return quarter		3,264
Dividend paid January 1986	46,000	
Add: ACT 3/7 × £46,000	19,714	

Franked payments	65,714
Excess of franked payments over FII	62,450
ACT payable 14 April 1986: 30% × £62,450	£18,735

Return quarter ended 30 June 1986
No relevant movements and no
return required

Return quarter ended 30 September 1986	£
FII received	1,920

Note:
A surplus of FII, being FII received £1,920, arises
in the AP ended 30 September 1986 because on
the change of ACT rate a notional AP for ACT
accounting only ends on 5 April 1986 (S.246(6),
TA 1988)

(ii) *Income tax accounting*

Return quarter ended 31 December 1985	£
Patent royalties paid 30 November 1985	6,150
Income tax payable 14 January 1986	1,845

Return quarter ended 31 March 1986	
Interest on government securities received	1,080
Income tax repayable £1,080 @ 30%	324

Return quarter ended 30 June 1986	
Patent royalties paid 31 May 1986	5,420
Interest on government securities received	1,320
	4,100
Income tax payable 14 July 1986 @ 29%	1,189

Return quarter ended 30 September 1986	
Interest on government securities received	1,600
Income tax repayable £1,600 @ 29%	464

(b) *AP ended 30 September 1986*
Capital allowances
Industrial buildings

	£
Residue at 1 October 1985	10,920
Proceeds June 1986	125,000
Balancing charge	£114,080
Restricted to allowance granted	£41,080

Note:
Roll-over of capital gain arising into new assets acquired in 12 months prior to sale.

New factory:

IA 25% × £138,000	34,500
WDA 4% × £188,000	7,520
	42,020

Corporation tax computation

Trading profit	66,456
Add: Depreciation	9,100
Balancing charge	41,080
Patent royalties	12,460
	129,096
Less: IBA	42,020
Schedule D Case I	87,076
UFII	4,000
Schedule D Case III	1,710
Total profits	92,786
Less: Charges – patent royalties paid	11,570
Profits chargeable	£81,216

Profits for small company rate purposes:

	£
Profits chargeable – income	81,216
FII	5,184
Profits for small company rate	£86,400

FY 1985 and 1986

Upper relevant amount $\dfrac{£500,000}{3} =$ £166,667

FY 1985 and 1986

Lower relevant amount $\dfrac{£100,000}{3} =$ £33,333

Corporation tax payable:

	£
1/2 × £81,216 @ 40%	16,243
1/2 × £81,216 @ 35%	14,213
	£30,456

Less marginal small companies relief:
FY 1985

$$1/2 \ (166,667 - 86,400) \times \frac{81,216}{86,400} \times \frac{1}{40} \qquad (943)$$

FY 1986

$$\frac{1}{2}(166{,}667 - 86{,}400) \times \frac{81{,}216}{86{,}400} \times \frac{3}{200}$$ (566)

£28,947

Less: ACT paid (less than
29.5% × £81,216)   18,735

Mainstream corporation tax   £10,212

Surplus FII
As per ACT accounting   1,920

(c)
Easton Ltd
Corporation tax computation
For the year ended 30 September 1986

	£	£
Schedule D Case I		26,820
Chargeable gain	5,880	
Apportioned to FY 1985	2,940	
Less: Abatement 1/4 × £2,940	735	
	2,205	
Apportioned to FY 1986 2,940		
Less: Abatement		
1/7 × £2,940 420	2,520	4,725
Total profits and profits chargeable		31,545
Corporation tax payable;		
Chargeable gains		
FY 1985 £2,205 @ 40%		882
FY 1986 £2,520 @ 35%		882
		1,764
Income		
1/2 × £26,820 @ 30%		4,023
1/2 × £26,820 @ 29%		3,889
		9,676
Less: ACT paid (less than 29.5% × £26,820)		707
Mainstream corporation tax		£8,969
Dividend paid	8,250	
Whereof under group election	6,600	
ACT paid 3/7 × (£8,250 − £6,600)	707	

(d) The loss of £71,200 in Avington Ltd for the 8 months ended
30 September 1986 may be relieved in the following ways:
  (i) It may be carried forward in Avington Ltd for set-off against
future profits of the same trade in Avington. This would delay

relief until corporation tax (if any) became payable in respect of the year ended 30 September 1988 – 30 June 1989, at the earliest. Any surplus of ACT arising from the dividend paid in 1983 is available for relief only if corporation tax were to arise in 1988 or subsequently. This would be a further reason for not claiming relief for the trading loss under S.393(1).

(ii) In view of losses in the year prior to the 8 months ended 30 September 1986, there is no possibility of obtaining loss relief by carry back under S.393(2). Likewise Avington has no other income in the 8 months against which to set the trading loss.

(iii) A proportion of the loss may be set off against a proportionate part of the profits of Itchen Ltd and Easton Ltd by way of group relief. The loss which may be surrendered is limited to the lesser of the loss and the profit available. Since Avington joined the Itchen group on 1 April 1986 the losses and profits available are:

	£
Avington	
Loss available 6/8 × £71,200	53,400
Itchen	
Profit available 6/12 × £81,216	40,608
Easton	
Profit available 6/12 × £31,545	15,772

The effect of claiming group relief would be to give earlier relief than that available by carry forward of the loss.

In Itchen's case, group relief of £40,608 would minimise the impact of the high marginal rate of tax that applies in Itchen to profits between £33,333 and £166,667. Application of the relief would restrict the ACT deductible. Notwithstanding this restriction, there is the possibility of carrying back the resulting surplus of ACT for 6 years in the case of this profitable company and obtaining possible early relief on carry forward. The balance of advantage would thus appear to lie with taking group relief first against the profits of Itchen Ltd to the maximum possible extent, and secondly against the profits of Easton Ltd.

Question 11

(a) *Dean Ltd*
Corporation tax computations
AP ended 31 March 1988

	£
Trading profit	3,386
Add: Leasing charges (see below)	3,018
Political donations	100
Increase in general provision – bad and doubtful debts	1,000

Legal fees – acquisition new lease	945
– factory disposal	3,720
Balancing charges – buildings	71,760
Depreciation	24,685
	108,614
Less: Profit on disposal of plant and machinery	(220)
Capital allowances – industrial buildings	(3,990)
– plant and machinery	(6,900)

Leasing charges:

$$£3,018 \times \frac{8,000 + (10,375 - 8,000)/2}{10,375}$$

	(2,672)
	94,832
Less: Losses brought forward (S.177(1))	94,832
	Nil
Building society interest	10,450
Chargeable gain	28,990
Total profits	39,440
Less: Charges	6,070
Profits chargeable	33,370
Corporation tax payable:	
£33,370 @ 35%	11,679.50
Less: ACT restricted to 27% of £33,370	9,009.90
	2,669.60
Less: Income tax on building society interest	2,821.50
Income tax repayment	151.90

(b)

	£
Adjusted trading profits as before	94,832
Add: Increase	150,000
	244,832
Less: Losses brought forward	98,878
Schedule D Case I	145,954
Building society interest	10,450
Chargeable gain (as before)	28,990
Total profits	185,394
Less: Charges	6,070
Profits chargeable	179,324

Lower relevant amount for marginal small companies relief:

$$\frac{£100,000}{2} \times \frac{3}{4}$$

£37,500

Upper relevant amount for marginal small
companies relief

$$\frac{£500,000}{2} \times \frac{3}{4} \qquad £187,500$$

Profits for marginal small companies relief:	
Profit chargeable to corporation tax	179,324
Add: FII	5,800
	185,124

Corporation tax payable:	
£179,324 @ 35%	62,763.40
Less: Marginal small companies relief:	

$$\frac{1}{40}(M - P) = \frac{1}{40}(187,500 - 185,124)$$

	59.40
	62,704.00
Less: ACT paid and surplus brought forward	11,448.00
	51,256.00
Less: Income tax – building society interest	2,821.50
Corporation tax payable	48,434.50

Capital allowances computation
Plant and machinery

	General pool (£)	Car pool (£)	Allowances (£)
WDV 1 July 1987	—	—	
Additions	22,760	14,540	
Disposals	(500)	—	
	22,260	14,540	6,900
WDA @ 25% × 3/4	(4,174)	(2,726)	
WDV 31 March 1988	18,086	11,814	
Total allowances			6,900

IBA		
Swindon factory		
AP ended 30 June 1979	£	£
Purchased July 1978		230,000
Less: land not available IBA		40,000
		190,000

Less: 30% offices not available IBA		57,00
Available IBA		133,00
Initial allowance 50%	66,500	
WDA 4%	5,320	71,82
Residue 30 June 1979		61,18
AP ended 31 March 1986		
WDA £5,320 × 3/4		3,99

Bristol factory

	£	£
AP ended 30 June 1981		
Purchased July 1980		130,00
Less: land not available IBA		38,00
		92,00
Initial allowance 50%	46,000	
WDA 4%	3,680	49,68
Residue 30 June 1981		42,32
AP ended 30 June 1982 to AP ended		
30 June 1987 – 6 years @ £3,680		22,08
Residue 30 June 1987		20,24
Sale price September 1987		200,28

Apportioned to land and to industrial
buildings on basis of cost:

Land $\frac{38}{130}$ × £200,280	58,543	
Industrial buildings $\frac{92}{130}$ × £200,280	141,737	141,737
	200,280	
Balancing charge		121,497
Restricted to allowances granted		71,760

Chargeable gain computation

	£
Disposal value of Bristol factory (September 1987)	200,280
Less: Purchase cost (July 1980)	(130,000)
Legal expenses of disposal	(3,720)
Gross gain	66,560
Indexation:	
March 1982 to September 1987:	
28.9% × 130,000	37,570
Chargeable gain	28,990

	£
ACT	
Franked payments:	14,600
Interim dividend	5,400
Add: ACT 27/73 × £14,600	
	20,000
	5,800
Less: FII	
	14,200
ACT @ 27%	3,834.00
Add: Surplus ACT brought forward	7,614.00
	11,448.00
	9,009.90
Less: Applied	
Surplus ACT carried forward	2,438.10

(c) *Bristol factory purchase*

(i) Residue after sale:

	£
Residue before sale	20,240
Add: Balancing charge	71,760
	92,000

Number of years still to run at September 1987 of 25 year period beginning July 1980 is 17 $^{10/12}$ years. On the assumption that the AP of the purchaser is 12 months, the WDA will be

$$\frac{1}{17^{10/12}} \times £92,000 = £5,159 \text{ annually}$$

	£	£
		92,000
(ii) Residue after sale		
2 years of use @ £5,159	10,318	
2 years of temporary disuse @ £5,159	10,318	
2 years of use @ £5,159	10,318	30,954
		61,046
Residue before sale		
Balancing charge restricted to on disposal		30,954
Balancing allowance unrestricted on disposal		

238 Solutions to questions

Question 12

Stratagem Ltd

Corporation tax computation
(a) *AP ended 31 March 1988*

	£
Schedule D Case I	
Trading income	546,000
Less: Capital allowances	17,800
	528,200
Schedule A	12,500
Schedule D Case III	640
Total profits	541,340
Charges – Debenture interest	6,000
Profits chargeable	535,340
Corporation tax payable:	
£535,340 @ 35%	187,369
Less: ACT	80,865
Mainstream corporation tax	106,504
Allowable capital loss carried forward	£1,476

Capital allowances computation
AP ended 31 March 1988

	General pool (£)	Car pool (£)	(1) Expensive car pool (£)	(2) Expensive car pool (£)	Total (£)
WDV 1 April 1987	44,800	15,700	10,100		
Additions				8,750	
	44,800	15,750	10,100	8,750	
Disposals	3,100	2,250			
	41,700	13,500	10,100	8,750	
WDA 25%	10,425	3,375	2,000*	2,000*	17,800
WDV 31 March 1988	31,275	10,125	8,100	6,750	
Total allowances					17,800

*Restricted

Allowable loss computation

	£
July 1987 – sale price of 5,000 shares Tactic Plc	5,200
March 1983 – purchase price	5,450

Gross loss	250
Indexation £5,450 × 0.225	1,226
Allowable loss carried forward	1,476

ACT

	£
Franked payments:	
2 August 1987 – £146,000 + 27/73 × £146,000	200,000
14 November 1987 – £73,000 + 27/73 × £73,000	100,000
Benefit in kind – shareholder £365 + 27/73 × £365	500
	300,500
FII:	
£730 + 27/73 × £730	1,000
Excess of franked payments	299,500
ACT @ 27%	80,865

(b) *Maximum relevant income*

	Total (£)	Estate (£)	Trading (£)	FII (net) (£)	UFII (£)
Schedule D Case I			528,000		
Schedule A		12,500			
UFII					640
FII				730	
	542,070	12,500	528,200	730	640
Charges	6,000	5,360			640
	536,070	7,140	528,200	730	—
C/T @ 35%	187,369	2,499	184,870	—	—
Distributable income	348,701	4,641	343,330	730	—
Lesser of £3,000 and 10% of estate or trading income				730	
Distributable investment income				Nil	
Less: Trading income		343,330			
Estate or trading income	4,641	Nil			
Maximum relevant income: 50% × £4,641 (Estate income)	2,320				

Question 13

(a) Q and T forms a 75% group and the trading losses of Q Ltd for the years ended 30 November 1987 and 1988 may be set off against the profits, as defined for group relief, of T Ltd.

Year ended 30 November 1987
T Ltd	£
Trading profit	10,000
Less: Loss brought forward (S.393(1))	5,000
	5,000
Schedule D Case III	5,000
	10,000
Less: Charges	2,000
	8,000
Less: Group relief claimed from Q Ltd	8,000
Profits chargeable	Nil

Q Ltd	£
Trading loss	12,000
Less: Surrendered to T Ltd	8,000
Loss carried forward (S.393(1))	4,000

Year ended 30 November 1988
T Ltd	£
Schedule D Case III	5,000
Less: Loss relief (S.393(2))	5,000
Trading loss	10,000
Less: Utilised (S.393(2))	5,000
Loss carried forward (S.393(1))	5,000
Add: Excess charges (S.393(9))	2,000
Total loss to be carried forward (S.393(1))	7,000

Q Ltd	£
Trading Loss	5,000
Add: Loss brought forward (S.393(1))	4,000
Loss carried forward (S.393(1))	9,000

Notes:
1. The profit of T Ltd available for group relief in the year ended 30 November 1987 is after deduction of trading losses brought forward. A claimant company's profits for relief are however

before deduction of losses from subsequent APs. There is therefore no need to apply T's loss for the next AP. Profits for group relief are *after* deduction of charges.

Application of group relief gives earlier relief than would application of S.393(2) relief (carry back against total profits) in respect of T Ltd's trading loss for the year ended 30 November 1988.

2. Unrelieved trading losses in each year are available for carry forward against future trading profits as are the excess trade charges which arise in T Ltd in the year ended 30 November 1988.

3. Claims for group relief must be made within 2 years of the end of the surrendering company's AP, and require its consent.

(b) Z Ltd is a consortium company and consortium group relief for trading losses is available as between the consortium company and the consortium members. Generally, a consortium company is a trading company owned at least to the extent of 75% by UK resident companies, none of whom own less than 5% of the ordinary share capital.

Year ended 30 June 1988

Profits of Z Ltd against which B Ltd's loss may be set off by way of group relief are:

	£
$\dfrac{24,000 \text{ shares}}{80,000 \text{ shares}} \times £50,000 =$	15,000
Less: Consortium group relief from B Ltd	15,000
	60,000
B Ltd Trading loss	15,000
Less: applied by way of group relief	
Loss carried forward (S.393(1))	45,000

Relief must be claimed within 2 years of the end of the AP of the surrendering company with the consent of the surrendering company and all other members of the consortium.

If the surrendering company is a member of the consortium only a fraction of the consortium company's profits, proportionate to the surrendering company's share in the consortium company, is available for relief.

APPENDIX 5

TABLE OF STATUTES

INDEX

252 *Index*